A novel by
Rajiv M. Vrudhula

SamSara

Phantazein
Press

PHANTAZEIN PRESS
Published by Phantazein Press
Chicago, Illinois
http://www.phantazeinpress.com

First American paperback edition
Published in 2000 by Phantazein Press

Copyright ©Rajiv M. Vrudhula, 1997
All rights reserved

ISBN 0-9676805-0-6
LCCN 99-068860
Printed in the United States of America

Acknowledgements

Very special thanks to my brother Sanjay and my sister Kalpana whose support helped to make this novel a reality. Special thanks also to Bill Delaney, Ameetha Palanki, and Beata Balogova without whose efforts this work would not have taken form. Many others must be mentioned: Adam Lowenstein, Kavita Daiya, and Sunita Sohrabji all read early drafts of this novel; their comments were essential to its further refinement. Vaishali Mahajan brought me to my first bhangra party in Chicago, an event which sparked this tale. Amit Kapur provided some of the details that have made this novel richer. I have received much encouragement and valuable critique before publication from a list of excellent readers: Alison Smith, Gouri Bhat, Sona Balazova, Dan Schulke, Tomasz Zorawski, Piotr Madej, Lise Shapiro, Eric Sanders, Anil Ramayya and Rich Lloyd. Finally, thanks to my parents Rayudu and Jaya for their faith in me throughout.

Book 1

1.

Jacob disbelievingly blinked and rubbed his eyes, already strained from hours of poring over the ancient religious text. Words were dancing on the page before him, joining together in ways pornographic to his disciplined mind. S's wrapped around t's, and v's opened to i's, giving birth to harsh-sounding strings of consonants. The letters began to form a distinguishable shape, and then faded again into a chaos of meaningless words. Could there really be something there? He pushed his chair back from the simple wooden desk. He stood up, stretched, and walked the nine or ten paces to his thin-mattressed bed, stepping over the books piled on his floor. He sat down and closed his eyes. "This is an impossibility," he said aloud, "A physical impossibility." Resting his eyes, he waited for his mind to clear. After a few minutes, he returned to his desk. Taking the book into his palms, he hoped to see words properly ordered on the page. But they began to move again.

Words had come to life: verbs actively skipped to their places, and nouns ponderously thudded along their appointed routes. Adjectives obsequiously followed their masters, while adverbs pirouetted alongside their companions. The rag-tag troops slowly took formation, halting after a short while. Trying to read the text, he brought his face closer to the page. Conjunctions clustered inconclusively, words split apart, letters illogically jumbled with one another. But a distinct shape was formed.

Jacob wanted to decode the logic of the letters and the words, or, what was left of them. He tried to read the letters backwards and forwards, left to right, right to left, upwards and downwards. He searched for a method to the ellipses, a sense of propriety amongst the twisted limbs and scrambled bodies that once formed sentences, but he found nothing, not a single distinguishable word, not a stray morpheme. No message was to be found. He was wasting precious time—the words began to move again. He sketched the symbol, taking each of the letters as points on various lines. Just as he finished, the process of disintegration accelerated, and words and letters took their former positions in sentences, leaving no trace of their mischief, save Jacob's hastily drawn sketch.

The next morning, Jacob sat at his desk, cradling an oversized mug of coffee. He breathed in the rich aroma of the dark brew, and then took a few careful sips. Pulling out a package of papers from his pocket, he expertly pinched a cigarette's worth of tobacco from the pouch set in front of him. After nimbly rolling his cigarette with his long, thin fingers, he lit it and began to smoke. Caffeine and nicotine. Addictions were luxuries, and these were the only two he allowed himself, since they both forced the body to keep pace with the mind. The first would hone his powers of concentration, which he would need now to make sense of the phenomenon he had witnessed the night before. The second would combat his nerves.

Now, what was he to do with this mystery? He closed the book and looked at its title: *The Book of Truth*. Ambitious. No, pretentious. "Well, I seemed to have found just what I needed. The answer to it all," Jacob said aloud to no one in particular, for there was no one to hear what he said. Well, there was *one*. Jacob was, for the most part, a solitary man. A scholar, a reader of books, a man of thought who publicly prided himself on his skepticism, and his deftly managed rationality. Yet also, a bookworm, a private dreamer, an erudite nonconformist. There were few he could still call his friends. He had no visitors, and his phone rarely rang.

He was not always so lonely. A student not so long ago, he had always been surrounded by people his age, all concerned with their intellectual pursuits. But Jacob left school, embarking upon his search alone, privately, without distractions and responsibilities. Since then, he read voraciously, consumed by a passion for learning. What was it he wanted to know? What drove him to his exegetical excesses, his avid bibliophilia, his reading until three o'clock in the morning and falling asleep with books piled on his body? Was it a repressed mania for myopia, a masochistic wish for other (metaphoric) children to throw (metaphoric) rocks at him on the (metaphoric) playground? A desire to remain forever physically clumsy, forever socially awkward?—all said to be the prices paid to achieve the multiple brain folds of the hyper-intelligent and hyper-studious. What exactly he was looking for he never knew, or really, could never say too well. So he read and read, each book itself being a snare for another ten, and in turn ten more. Doing the math—there was an exponential increase into infinity in the offing. "God in the details, devil in the footnotes," his professor of biblical hermeneutics told him once. And Jacob's devil lured him ever further and further away from what was once his life, on a lonely path for knowledge. So the once awkward and shy man with few friends, became even more isolated, lost in his books, ever searching for something.

Could he have been kept off the path of loneliness? Were there no friends to throw a rope to him down that bottomless well he had hurled himself into, to pull him out to speak to him of love and sex, of flowers and earth, and death and starry nights? Or at least to go to a movie? Even an art film, yes, even a sixties experimental art film would have enlivened him. There were friends once. There were discussions, arguments, debates on all the finer points of philosophy over beer and pizza. One friend even counseled against leaving school, "School keeps things in perspective, Jacob. You could get lost in your head. A bitter, anti-social auto-didact." To this same friend, just as their friendship began to fade with unreturned phone calls and broken social arrangements, Jacob said, "Don't you see the value of all of this—the value of all of these words, these books, the pursuit of knowledge itself? To be able to create a world with books, with words, to see the world as others see it, to interpret and understand? That's why we do what we do." It was an impassioned speech, and almost spontaneous—Jacob had imagined his delivery of it for weeks beforehand. A "give me liberty or give me death" would have been a nice touch...Perhaps not. But still, he lost contact with his friends. And communication with his family was infrequent, and concentrated only on vital statistics: No, he did not have a job. No, he was not going back to Divinity School. No, he did not have a girlfriend. Yes, his reading was going just fine, thanks for asking.

It would be wrong to belittle his project, whatever it was exactly. It was after all, something like the noble goal of Western thought, the progression of rationality from Plato to Descartes and beyond, from the Classical Age to Enlightenment. From metaphysics to the Industrial Revolution. To rocket science. To plastic. To lycra. More than all of that, Jacob had a desire to know things, to understand the world around him, and the thoughts of people alive a thousand years ago, to enter into their minds and wander about, searching and evaluating. In short, he had the desire for God, the God of philosophers. There was no devilish hand involved after all. Solitude was required for this quest, and loneliness was the price to be paid.

Jacob was startled by the pain of sharp pins and a light weight on his shoulder. Turning his head, he gently lifted his Egyptian hairless –the "one" referred to above– by the neck and held him over the book.

"Well, Nicodemus, what do you think about all of this? Just listen to the subtitle: "A Translation of a sacred text of a Tantrik sect of the ancient land of India. By Francis Stoutheart."

"Meow." Cat eyes stared down to the book ad then back at Jacob. Nicodemus, too, was curious and perhaps a little tense.

Francis Stoutheart. Jacob thought to himself. Who was he? Scholar? Civil Servant? One of the legendary surveyors of the Company? A stray adventurer, maybe, with a hunger for discovery and exploration. Long ago travelling to India to find excitement, to earn the mantle of manhood by taming the wily Orient. One thing was for certain. The book represented years of labor. Whoever he was, Stoutheart had dedicated a significant part of his life to translating this book, and what a book it was! Exactly one thousand pages, full of magical incantations, elaborately detailed rituals, and a host of philosophical essays treating everything from questions of reincarnation, to the mind-body problem, to the substance and nature of consciousness. Two days Jacob had spent enamored by its explanations and postulations, and its descriptions of tantric sexual practices and mantras. Jacob had never seen anything like it before. He had never heard of Stoutheart, but "tantra" was a word he had heard. It had been mentioned in passing in the various academic and intellectual circles that he had once frequented, but he had never paid much attention when it was. In his mind the word was associated with a class of people, vaguely imagined to be living in California somewhere, who advocated the ideas and practices of the New Age: pyramid power, crystal consultation, anus-sunning and the consumption of large amounts of organic wheat bulgur.

He opened the cover and read the first page:

Upon returning from our adventure, it became clear that committing to print in our own Language the words of the unknown author or authors would serve the pursuit of Knowledge most efficaciously. That the esteemed reader will bring Erudition and Judgement to bear in this matter, we most certainly hope, for it is in such a way that Providence will provide a guiding hand in ascertaining that which is True, and that which is False. And it is through the knowledge of falsity that the cause of Truth may be upheld.

Jacob had paid little attention to these words when he was first given the book three days before. They seemed innocent enough. But the short note, written on what was now a tattered, yellowed paper and placed inside the book jacket concerned him now.

My dear Samuel,

I have only now gained enough courage to put this work into circulation. I have been plagued by the most uncertain anxieties, irrepressible appetites, and outlandish dreams since the day I began translating it. I have left out the ominous incantation that appears in the original. You may recall that it threatens retribution by the Tantra-dasi Sabha. *They must be a secret society of some sort, perhaps some kind of Guardians of the Book. It is of course not surprising that in such a barbarous, secretive land such threats would be made to strike fear in the hearts of the superstitious. As you well know, I think nothing of their superstitions, but there is still the matter of these dreams. And a most remarkable, troubling thing has happened with this book that I am sending to you. I cannot say what it is, I can only ask that you examine it thoroughly. We still have a chance to discuss all of these matters soon enough, as I am awaiting your arrival here.*

Francis

Jacob reviewed the facts that he possessed. Not a scientist, but not a stranger to scientific thinking, Jacob thought highly of the results achieved by the application of calm, rational thinking in irrational situations. He was scared a bit—he did not question his own sanity. But perhaps, he thought, he had been spending far too much time alone in the last year or two. The mind could play the strangest of tricks to warn itself of imminent breakdown. But back to the facts. Fact one: Jacob possessed an obscure work—a translation of an even more obscure religious text. A text that named no date or place of publication or a name of publisher. That's not too unusual. It looked at least a hundred years old, judging from its condition. Though indeed it could have been twice that age. (So far Jacob remained calm, without the tell-tale signs of anxiety attack. No narrowing of vision, no sweaty palms. Yet). An obscure book. Nothing at all unusual about that. Libraries were full of forgotten books, read by only a handful of people long ago. Next fact. (This particular set of facts was looking to contain less information than he had hoped a calm replay of evidence might. Back on track). The note from Stoutheart to his friend. An unknown scholar writes a hasty letter to a friend to accompany a rare and obscure book. Nothing odd about that, except perhaps the air of panic only slightly concealed under a thin veil of gentility. Samuel—the friend in question—was to visit Stoutheart. Somewhere. Sometime. That was all. What became of them? The meeting? Stoutheart? Samuel? Who were these Guardians of the book? What were these dreams that must have woken up poor Stoutheart in the middle of the night? And what was the troubling thing that had happened with the book? Jacob lost peripheral vision, and his hands began to sweat. On the verge of an anxiety attack—he thought about the next "fact": Words had moved upon the page, forming this symbol he had sketched. He had never seen it before—it hadn't sprung from his imagination. It *had* happened. *It really had happened.*

Jacob stood in front of his bathroom mirror, lathering his face for a shave. He was going to see the Librarian today. Three days ago he had met him. Those fascinating days had been spent immersed in esoteric Eastern Knowledge. In the library, Jacob was taking one of his usual trips browsing for books. He walked through the intricate maze of bookstacks, not seeing any one else as he wandered. He lost track of time, unsure how long he had been there. He had lost his way and began to feel a daze, a disorientation settle upon his mind. His sure-footed gait soon gave way to a stumble in the dimly lit corridors. The stacks themselves seemed to guide him, shifting and forcing him to follow a particular direction. The maze seemed to grow more and more complex. Finally, when the passageway began to straighten, he could make out a yellowish glow at its end. As Jacob approached the light, the outlines of a desk appeared. A small man took shape behind the desk as Jacob came closer and closer. It must have been the dim light, but he seemed to have appeared and not have been there before. Who was he? Why was he here? A Librarian, Jacob surmised. But more than the mere cataloguer and caretaker of books, he was the keeper of the ideas contained within them.

The man behind the desk spoke. "Can I help you find something?" he asked, his head slightly bowed. Jacob came closer and stood just a few feet away from him. He was a lean man, wearing a brown wool sweater. His slightly sweat-moistened head reflected the light from his desk lamp. He had set his hands on the desk, interlacing his thin fingers.

"Just browsing," Jacob finally managed to say, combating both a parched throat and the inexplicable stupor into which he had fallen. He had said it only out of habit. That his first words to the man who would very soon become his guru, his spiritual master and guide, were the same spoken to department store sales clerks Jacob would never forgive himself. "I think I've taken a wrong turn...." he continued. Sincere reflection lay behind his next words, as Jacob looked around uneasily. "It's a little dark in here."

The small man flashed his grey, penetrating eyes at Jacob, and then smiled slightly. It was a kind smile, though it lasted only a short moment. "Follow me," he instructed. The old man turned to unlock the door behind him. Jacob quickly maneuvered around the desk so as not to risk being left behind. They entered the door, and walked through yet another series of book-lined passageways, connected by dank and dark hallways and staircases. Several minutes later, Jacob stood alongside his guide in front of a chain-linked fence door that led to a further series of shelves and dark corridors. "I'm in charge of this collection," the Librarian said in a low voice. "Occult Sciences." He unlocked the door. And as they walked onwards, the older man continued to speak. "Here, look. Black Magic. White Magic. Demonism," he said, pointing to volumes of musty-smelling books. "Crowley, *The Necronomocon*... How about Cabala? Do you have a taste for secret societies? Rosicrucians? Templars? I have an entire section on Christian heretics. Gnostics maybe? Or are pagan rituals more your style?" His eyes alighted with enthusiasm when he said "pagan rituals". "Druids, cults of Bacchus, Odin, Osiris, Isis? Here we are, Hittites, Sumerians, Zoroastrians..." R's rolled as he spoke. "Mayans, Aztecs," he continued. "Buddhism: Mayahana or Theravada..." H's were heavy and breathy. "...Tame stuff. The Tibetans, on the other hand, livened things up with a little dash of Bon. Here, Vedic hymns, Upanishads—no collection is complete without them. Bhakti and sufi poetry. Yoga? Aryan horse sacrifice? Kali or Siva cults?"

Jacob was supposed to answer, to make a decision, to choose from amongst the options available to him. To choose a secret knowledge and art to master. "I just don't know about all of this...It's not what I had in mind." Despite his curiosity, Jacob refused the offer and turned to walk away. How he would get out, he had not yet determined. He had to leave this bewildering place, which frightened him, but which he found so strangely attractive.

"Take this one," the Librarian said in the same low voice of command he had used to entice Jacob to follow him. "I think you might find it interesting." Jacob turned around to face him. His small eyes were purposefully staring, opened as widely as they could be.

Now, days later, standing in front of his bathroom mirror shaving, Jacob made a decision. He was going to speak to the Librarian. Find out more information. Even risk ridicule by telling him what happened. Certain that he would not be taken seriously, Jacob had already crawled back into bed three times, placed pillow over forehead, and repeated aloud two phrases. "I have to do this." and "They'll think you're crazy." The first impulse won out when he decided to visit, though he resigned himself to the status of space alien abductees. Jacob did not often talk to himself aloud—though his conversations

with Nicodemus could be considered somewhat one-sided.
But certainly under the circumstances, a case of nerves could
be excused.

He shaved badly, cutting himself. He looked his reflection over in the mirror. He was not an unattractive man. Thin
and lanky, but not especially weak. Perhaps a little pale.
Maybe it was lack of sunlight, or overexposure to the flores-
cent light of his desk lamp. He tried to comb his short brown
hair, trying to battle its perennial dishevelment. He flexed his
muscles, sucked in his stomach. He ran his fingers through
his hair hoping they might be more successful at imposing
order than his comb. He leaned into the mirror and looked
closely at his teeth. Frustrated, he comforted himself with the
thought that there were those who would find his slight
neglect of body to be charming, a mark of serious intellect.
(And there would be. At least one. No, there would be three!)
He sighed. He never seemed to find the time to discover if
that were true. Here he was, he told himself, an average
looking man with an average body that carried within it an
intensely curious and passionate intellect. The body had to be
denied for the mind. Iron abdominals and tight ass be
damned.

Nicodemus hopped onto Jacob's shoulder. A member of a
particularly agile breed, Nicodemus had perfected the floor to
shoulder jump from a full-rest position. What the Egyptian
hairless possessed in agility, it lacked in beauty. Gray, hairless
elastic skin folded around his neck and eyes. It was not true
that Jacob chose Nicodemus to make himself look more
attractive. He was, in fact, allergic to cat hair. He was able to
defray the cost of his companion with a student loan, redi-
rected after his visit to the Dean's office to withdraw.

Finally dressed in jeans and yellow t-shirt, single color no
insignia, and after one more debate with himself whether or
not he should go, Jacob made his final decision—it could not
be any other way—and asked Nicodemus to wish him well.
The feline, claws extended and front paws striking through the
air, was battling with unseen spirits and paid little attention to

his departing master. Feeling a little snubbed, Jacob locked his apartment door and headed for the bus stop, his sketch neatly folded and tucked in his jean's pocket.

An unremarkable man in a bustling city walked along the crowded sidewalks, bracing himself to tell a most remarkable story.

Jacob once again stood before the mysterious Librarian, guided to him by one of the library's bespectacled book shelvers. The small man smiled in recognition, and Jacob nodded in response to the silent greeting. Still smiling to hide his nervousness, Jacob pulled out a folded piece of paper from his pocket, opened it and handed it to the old man.

"Do you recognize this?"

"Of course I do," said the Librarian, barely glancing at Jacob's sketch, and not making any motion to take the proffered paper. "It's a mandala. A tantric mandala—a sacred symbol."

"I copied it from the book you gave me a few days ago." Jacob had hoped for the Librarian to respond knowingly, to offer an explanation for the book's misbehavior. But he did not comply.

"Nice work." He looked over the drawing again, almost carelessly. "But the lines are a little shaky."

"I don't think you understand—"

The Librarian raised his hand, with his palm facing Jacob. "Of course I do."

"No, look, this might sound a little odd. I came here because, well, to tell you that-that the book you gave me, it possesses, possesses some mechanism or something that creates the illusion—yes—it must be an optical illusion—that the letters and words can move." Jacob stuttered onwards, hoping for a rational explanation, "And once this *illusion* of motion stops, well, they, the letters I mean, seem to suggest the appearance of this....this....mandala, and..."

The old man interrupted him. "Words in motion?" he asked. Did he speak in disbelief? Jacob could not tell. The

Librarian continued to smile his kind, knowing smile, his face too calm to reveal what he might think of Jacob's story. And Jacob, having finally told someone what happened began to feel his skepticism return. If his story was not to be believed by others, than Jacob himself would begin to dismantle it.

"Yeah, words in motion. Do you have any idea what the symbol might mean? It's not like any of the others in the book—the normal drawings..."

"It's meaning? That is a difficult question. A very difficult question. Can I interest you in something else?" the Librarian asked, grandiosely waiving his arm, gesturing to no book in particular, but to all of them. "I have elegant metaphysical treatises...How's your Latin? Aaaah... and the most moving meditations on death, dying, love, living...." he said wistfullly. He stood up from his desk chair, and turned to open the door behind him. "Let me see here....." He walked through the doorway, and Jacob followed him. The Librarian maintained a surprising speed, and Jacob struggled to keep pace.

Speaking from several feet behind him, Jacob called out, "I don't think you understand...That's not what I'm asking..."

The Librarian stopped abruptly and turned around and smiled. "You're right. You don't seem to be in the right frame of mind for this kind of thing. How about something happy? Hmm? A little upbeat?"

"Please look at this. Tell me what it means." Jacob thrust out the piece of paper, but the Librarian refused to take it a second time.

"I admire your persistence." He turned around again, and resumed his quick-paced walk, with Jacob following behind him. They reached a second fenced door, which Jacob had not passed through the first time he had seen the Librarian. "Let's go in here and have a little talk."

The Librarian sat Indian style, as it were, on a small Oriental rug set in a dark, mostly empty alcove just inside the door. The walls looked like they could be moldy, but only seemed so because of the dim light. In truth, they were frequently scrubbed clean. Jacob sat facing him, uncomfortable, his legs folded and crossed as well. The elder man lit a small brass oil lamp, and then pinched some tobacco from a pouch set on the bare concrete floor to the side of the rug, and placed it in a small hookah. He lit the pipe, and began to smoke. After several minutes, he offered Jacob a puff, but he politely refused, and pulled out his own pouch of tobacco and papers. He rolled a cigarette and began to smoke also. The two men sat in a reflective silence, the air around them filling with dreamy tobacco smoke.

"You see, Jacob," the Librarian finally said, "you have been chosen by the Book. Chosen. It has led you here to me. You see, it is a magical book." And then he put the hookah's tube to his mouth, sucking in air and smoke, causing the water inside of it to gurgle vigorously.

"Magical. Right. Magic ending with a "k" I take it," Jacob said sarcastically.

"If you doubt, why are you here? There is a place for doubt, Jacob. I was young like you once –a boy– always asking questions. A skeptic. But you saw something with your own eyes...It is true, the senses may deceive. But your curiosity brought you here. So, somewhere within yourself you must believe."

"I'm curious, that's true. But I'm also skeptical."

"Keep your skepticism, Jacob. But do not let it prevent you from seeing things that you might otherwise see." Jacob nodded, thinking over the old man's words. They smoked more, while Jacob's minded wandered. He wondered what price he had paid for his doubt and disbelief, and if these characteristics were even true of him. When had it all began?

"I am master of a Tantric Order, Jacob," the Librarian announced abruptly. "The Book has chosen you. I have chosen you. I ask you to join us, to learn from us what you can. But Jacob, if you refuse to join us, you must never tell anyone of our existence. We are a secret order, Jacob. We have made many sacrifices to survive, and we have survived through years upon years of isolation and banishment through secrecy. You must tell no one what you have heard so far, nor what I am about to tell you."

And with that, Jacob was told many wondrous things. He heard tales of long-haired seers, and forest sages around whom trees would grow as they meditated for years upon years. Of secret societies and priests and devotees of one god or another. Stories of glorious, ineffable ecstasies, and the most severe and painful of asceticisms. The Librarian revealed the origins of Tantra, that religion of pleasure for the sake of salvation, whose practitioners sought power through indulgence of the body. Some even sought spiritual power by cultivating the base emotions of hate and anger. He was told of outlaw sages, renegades amongst renegades, hounded from their ashrams for their heresies. Some of these holy men hid themselves in the wilds. Some left their homelands so they could practice their forbidden arts, spreading their secrets only to a select few. The Librarian tended his hookah all the way through, he and Jacob both providing the ambient smoke. There were also theft and betrayals by explorers, treasure-seekers interested only in peddling the secret knowledge of the East. And there were the enemies from within the sects, the power-hungry, the schism-mongerers, the traitors. Thousands of years ago, ashram mates had come to blows over the best way to access the great source of cosmic energy. Hair was pulled, punches were thrown, and a few unlucky ones were thrown from precipices into impossible chasms. This was the First Schism. One group emerged victoriously, and the sect grew and grew in numbers, and evolved through the ages, changing in whatever ways that were necessary to maintain its truth, and, its secrecy. It found a home in this Library many years ago, with this small man as its quiet teacher and all-powerful leader.

Jacob sat through at rapt attention, never interrupting, moving only to shift his weight or to roll another cigarette. When the Librarian had finally finished speaking, whether he was too tired to go on or simply no longer wished to continue Jacob did not know, he said to him, "You must come tomorrow, and we shall begin with your lessons. But, now, follow me. There is one more thing you should see."

Jacob followed the Librarian for several minutes through the main corridor of the Occult Sciences section, which soon opened up into a much larger hall. At the opposite end and furthest away from where Jacob had entered stood a wall of cubicles. Pairs of dread-locked, loin-clothed men and women occupied many of these cells, while others were singly inhabited. Many were practicing intricate yogic postures, while some sat with only legs crossed. All chanted the sacred syllable "OM," creating a solemn buzzing sound that reverberated through the hall. And at least three pairs of the devotees were managing copulation, along with the performance of the most physically demanding yogic exercises. One man stood upon a single hand, thrusting his pelvis into a twisted pretzel of a woman, her arms where legs should have been. Or was she thrusting her pelvis? Hard to tell. Neither this particular couple nor any of the others paid attention to the thin, young man, mouth agape, staring at them, unable to turn away, too embarrassed to blush, too captivated to move or speak.

"They're perfecting the asanas—the manipulations of the body that can lead to spiritual bliss. We are, unfortunately, experiencing a shortage of partners for many of them," the Librarian explained.

How long did Jacob stand there watching, learning, fascinated with the unlimited possibilities available to the properly flexible human body? It may have been fifteen minutes, or it may have been an hour. It was beyond pornography for Jacob, less and more than art—he felt the cosmic energy, he felt the indescribable lure of the Tantric Way. He felt as though he should have dated more often in college. At last, the Librarian broke the spell as he gently tugged Jacob on the arm to leave. Jacob's unasked questions: "Do we have to go? Can I watch a little longer? Is all of this really possible? And, just how does that dreadlocked blonde managed to do that while balancing on the top of her head?"

"Don't you tell nobody about nothing!" someone shrilly screamed from behind Jacob, bringing him to shame for his voyeurism. He turned to see an unremorsefully pudgy and pale nude man, his hair bundled on the top of his head. A swastika was painted on his forehead. "Nobody doesn't know nothing about this nowhere! Nothing to nobody!" he shouted at Jacob, shaking his index finger back and forth, spraying droplets of saliva into Jacob's face. Not prepared for confrontation, and feeling rightly rebuked for his lasciviousness, Jacob was left flustered and speechless by the soft-bellied sadhu.

"Leave him alone, Brother Govind," admonished the Librarian, staring into the naked man's reddened face. Stepping aside and displaying a servile grin, he responded, "As you wish, guru." And then Govind stuck his tongue out until its tip touched his chin—a relic from the cult's Tibetan exile ages ago—in respectful farewell to his master.

When they were well clear of the plump Govind, the Librarian half-whispered to Jacob, "Don't mind him. He has chosen a fruitless path," he confided. "The Via Negativa he calls it. His mission is to bring the double negative into English. And through this negation –poof– Nirvana. What foolish nominalism! But, Jacob, let me tell you, whatever his faults, he has helped us a great deal."

When they returned to the first gate that led to the secret hideaway of the Order, Jacob took leave of the Librarian. Fascinated by what he had seen and heard, he promised to return the next day to begin his lessons. And with that promise, Jacob, the self-proclaimed skeptic, the scholar, yes, that Jacob, had joined a cult.

2.

*e*ach afternoon for at least a week, Jacob engaged in his own private ritual of denial. After returning home from his morning meetings with the Librarian, he would sit with Nicodemus in his lap, and say to him, "Hello, cat. I've gone crazy. I've joined a cult. I'm a member of a cult. Yes, that's right, a cult. I'm a cultie." Yet, the next morning of each of the following days, he would tell Nicodemus while coffee brewed, "Look, cat. You saw for yourself what the book did. Besides, that's not important. I'm learning something new...And it's not a cult," he would rationalize. "He doesn't want anything from me. I haven't shaved my head. I haven't given him everything I own. He doesn't drive a Mercedes Benz. He's only my guru. Yeah, I know what you're thinking, cat. I'm a prime candidate for cult recruitment. Lonely drop-out virgin who talks to his cat. But this is different. What's the point!" he would finally say, exasperated "You just wouldn't understand!" And Nicodemus, with the cold eyes of an assassin, would only respond by diving through the air while hissing at ghosts.

Jacob's skepticism seemed to fade as he allowed himself to learn from the Librarian. And learn he did—ideas and words that were so distant and foreign became familiar, and the familiar became strange and took on new meaning. Breathing itself he rediscovered—for it had to be done with concentration upon the sacred syllable "OM," the very basis for life, and the beginning point for meditation. Jacob would spend entire days sitting with the Librarian in his alcove, simply breathing, focusing on the syllable, maintaining a profound silence, a mental blankness, for as long as he could. Such a serenity he had never known. An anxiety, born from the nervousness of knowing too little, and the race to know more, had always driven him before. But now, all that he needed to understand was contained in the "OM" and the power of the breath.

Soon the Librarian told Jacob of the structure of the subtle body—not a mere mass of blood and tissue, muscle and bone, it was the place for flows of energy, composed of the chakras. And within that subtle body, lurked a powerful snake, seated at the base of the spine. This snake was the secret of the kundalini. To awaken it, to cause it to spring upwards was to release tremendous spiritual energy, which was required for liberation. "Freedom from what?" Jacob asked. The Librarian simply smiled and said, "From all of this, Jacob. Life and death. And your endless, painful desires."

It was because of these lessons that Jacob quickly came to love the Librarian. The hallowed, age-old bond between teacher and student, master and disciple, *guru* and *chela*, was such a powerful one because it is based on that great gift: knowledge. And Jacob was hungry for knowledge, though he finally found a kind of learning that did not create an empti- ness, but which filled him with a sense of serenity. And it was for this peace that Jacob revered his teacher, who gave to him so selflessly.

Yet, oddly enough, and the question did cross Jacob's mind once or twice, despite all the tantric philosophising, very little was said about sex.

One day, several weeks after his first meeting with the Librarian, Jacob found himself walking down the street, clutching an address for a cafe in his right hand, and another book given to him by his spiritual teacher in his left. He wasn't sure why he was told to go to this cafe—he was not given a name, only a quickly scribbled address. The Librarian had simply told him that there were two others he was to meet. Two very powerful members of the Order, unlike any of the others. Powerful. Dangerous. Rash. These were the words he used. But he also told Jacob, "I have great respect for them, and you should too. They can teach you many things, but you must resist their temptations. Be strong Jacob, and you will learn much, much more, when it is time. But be careful, be very careful." His last words were like those of a father to a son leaving home for the first time—full of understanding, faith, and sorrow. But is it wrong to sentimentalize a man who led a small army of fornicating fakirs? This question Jacob would never ask himself, despite what would happen to him.

Now apprehensive, and nervous, Jacob strolled aimlessly to calm himself and to take a moment for reflection before hailing a taxi cab. The Librarian had seemed such a gentle, humble soul, but Jacob had already seen the extent of his power. He had followers. Devotees. Acolytes who paid the utmost deference to him and his word. It was incredible! True, Jacob had "joined" the Order, but he had only really seen the others on the first day, when he was shown the cubicles. He had been separated from them for special instruction, though Jacob did not realize the honor it was to be taught by the Librarian in private. Well, he may have, but he would never say so. He felt no kinship to his supposed peers, though indeed he felt an almost filial loyalty to the Librarian. For the rest, he was only amazed with their apparent devotion, and with their discipline. They were living the words spoken by their mild, tender teacher.

Now, when Jacob remembered his purpose, remembered the paper in his hand, he felt his apprehension return. He also had no luck in flagging a cab, since he had been standing on the curb, with his head bowed in thought. He was to see two more members of the Order—and they seemed to worry the Librarian, or really, make the old man worry for Jacob's sake.

"Taxi! Taxi! he shouted, waiving the piece of paper in the air. At last successful, a cab pulled up in front of him. He opened the door, got in, and called out the address to the driver.

"Share a cab?" a man in an olive-colored, well-tailored business suit brusquely asked Jacob before he closed the door, and sat beside him. "You're heading in my direction," he said, pointing to the sheet of paper in Jacob's hand and then slamming the cab door shut.

The pushy businessman and his somewhat bewildered-looking cabmate were picked up by one Afziz Ahmed, licensed taxi driver number AF34786, recent emigre from Pakistan, and resident of the westside Indo-Pak neighborhood, along with his brothers Aijaz and Khalil.

"Hey Affsays, get a move on it!" shouted Olive-suit, noticing the driver's name on the cab permit. The picture seemed only to vaguely resemble the living man. Hollow, expressionless eyes stared out from the i.d. card on the dashboard, and a four-day-old beard growth prevented an accurate reading of facial features. Ambiguity defined the picture's very essence. What nefarious criminal activity would such a photo be part of would be discovered not many weeks later by a sympathetic black-haired beauty. At least for the present passengers, the picture convincingly fit the man, even though the flesh and blood Afziz was proudly clean-shaven. The only shadow on his dark brown-skinned face occurred at certain times of day, when the sun beamed upon his exceptionally large nose. And he had much more hair than the short-haired Afziz portrayed in the photo. One might observe that the almost greasy, messy hair that topped Afziz's head assumed its present posture not from neglect, but from an inherent waviness that resisted the civilizing mission of the comb, embodying a South Asian defiance to Western bourgeois civility. But the truth was that Afziz had overslept that morning, swore and screamed at his brothers for not awakening him from his nap after morning prayers, and ran from his house unsatisfactorily groomed—he did shave, however; he always shaved. But time was money in this business. To make amends for his appearance, Afziz buttoned his blue plaid shirt up to the top button, tucked it into his blue jeans, and impulsively attempted, at every stoplight and stop sign, to smooth his hair.

Speaking in his accented Pakistani-English, Afziz protested to Olive-suit, "I'm trying my best sir. I'm knowing a short-cut—you're getting there in a jiffy."

"Great. A jiffy. You better watch these damn shortcuts of yours—" The man turned to Jacob, and smiled, seeking an ally. "Hey! What the hell are you doing, cabbie? What the hell are you going down this street for?"

Afziz was in no mood for such petulance today. "I'm losing my patience...I am no one to be pushed over! In Islamabad, I killed six people! Six people! I cannot return there." Afziz was known by his brothers to stretch the truth sometimes, but they knew his standard response to bother-some customers. Aijaz would often ask, "But, Afziz, my brother, does it have to be six? They are already thinking that we are tying dynamite to our babies and putting them in the trunks of autos. And Afziz, you know they cannot tell a Pakistani from a Palestinian." And Afziz would respond, "Yes, my brother, it must be six. You know six has always been a lucky number for me. Remember, I am the sixth child of our beloved father, who was the sixth child of his father. Without the number six, I would not be here."

Jacob gripped the door handle nervously when told of the six. How Afziz killed them, he did not know...in one of their countless wars, in some dark, treacherous Asian alley for some despicable criminal purpose, or even some horrid driving accident that forced Afziz to flee Pakistani justice—would they hang him? How could Olive-Suit antagonize him so!

"All right buddy. Whatever you say. Just don't go taking anymore of your goddamned shortcuts, or you can kiss your tip adios!"

"You didn't hear what he said, did you?" Jacob whispered.

"What? No, I never listen to these guys." He looked at Jacob, once ally, now meddler, and then he looked at the book in Jacob's hand. *Meditative Practices for Communication with Superplanar Beings.* "Anyway, what's it to you?"

"Six people, I killed six people. They will arrest me if I return!" Afziz continued to mutter.

After sharply turning round a corner, Afziz slammed on his brakes to avoid hitting a group of robe-clad, head-shaved jaywalkers. "Hare Krishna! Hare Rama!" they cried, oblivious to traffic.

"A bloody degeneration of morals! It is getting so that you cannot tell a proper Hindu these days." Afziz shouted. "It has always been difficult, but now! Ah! I will teach these frauds a lesson!" And with that, Afziz honked his horn, and forced his cab through the throng. Alarmed Hare Krishnas, increasing the tempo of their "Hare Rama-Hare Krishna" chant in a panic, ran or leapt for safety.

A few minutes later, Afziz pulled the cab in front of an ornately decorated building, stone lions guarding the entrance, and waited for Jacob to get out.

"Are you sure this is the place?" asked Jacob, eyeing the Corinthian columns and the two seated, but roaring, stewards.

"It is the address on the paper. This is the correct destination. Please pay the proper fare plus twenty per cent tip and exit the vehicle from the door closest to the curb," instructed Afziz, pointing to the notice affixed to the back seat passenger window.

"You're certain?" Jacob looked at the bright neon sign above entranceway. Cafe Feu d'Amour. Hard for him to believe that he would be sent here.

"Yes, I am quite certain. Now pay, and then you must leave. Your friend here is getting most impatient."

Jacob paid his share, got out of the cab, and closed the door behind him. Had he turned around, he might have seen the anger in Afziz's squinted eyes, the predatory visage of an overworked taxi driver pushed too far. But Jacob should have guessed at Afziz's mood from the way he slammed on the accelerator, peeling out with an ear piercing squeal. Olive-suit's head was thrown back, though he maintained his smile. A car wreck meant that he could sue. And it was all the better that the Pakistani was moving a little faster. He was well-used to the hunter's bloodthirsty glare, so he saw Afziz's threat as a manageable challenge. He would fondle the three hundred dollar pen in his jacket pocket for the rest of the ride, remaining calm, not showing any fear for his safety.

Jacob entered the cafe through the revolving doors. Lamps hung low from the ceiling, their light seeming to bleed because of the thick cigarette smoke. Portraits of naked men and women engaged in various sexual acts, modeled after the erotic temple sculptures of Khajurao, served as the ceiling and wall moldings. A few bulbously bellied Happy Buddhas were thrown in here and there amongst the lovers to satisfy demands for equal access. Marbletop tables were surrounded by well-padded antique chairs, and brushed-velvet booth seats lined the walls. There was not an empty table to be seen, and no one looked as if they were going to leave. It was a place where patrons settled for hours, reading, or playing chess or backgammon, sipping cappucino after cappucino, followed by a fine brandy.

From across the room, a man motioned for Jacob. Excusing himself at least six times, and earning both smiles and frowns as a result, Jacob finally succeeded in negotiating through the crowded cafe and reached the seat reserved for him.

"I've been expecting you," said the man, surprising Jacob with the graveness of his tone. "My name is Aloysius Caine." He stood up abruptly, pushing his seat back as he did, and then firmly grasped Jacob's hand in greeting. "Sit down, Jacob. Please." Aloysius was a muscular man, a few years older than Jacob. He wore a tight black t-shirt, black jeans, and his hair was closely cropped. Once Jacob sat down, Aloysius, out of nervous habit, raised his left hand and tugged at his gold earring with index finger and thumb. Then he lifted his hand into the hair, and held up two fingers. The two men sat in silence until a waiter brought two espressos.

"Do you know why you have been sent to me?" He paused, waiting for Jacob to answer. But Jacob didn't respond, unable to match the other man's intensity. "I am to teach you some very important things." He paused again, but this time he was not waiting for a reply. "Are you ready?" Jacob nodded. "Good. I use the power of *anger* to tread the path of salvation," he said, in a low, conspicuously controlled tone. He was struggling to maintain composure, to keep himself from shouting.

Jacob sipped the last of his espresso from his tiny cup, and diplomatically asked, "Why are you angry?"

"I am angry because life is not what it could be. I am angry because we lie to one another. And because I am misunderstood. They stare at me, always, they are staring at me, but never can they see what is inside."

Jacob took a closer look into the face of his interlocutor. He was a man whose physical strength and presence made him handsome; his chiselled jawline and cleft chin suggested his determination. But his hazel eyes were bloodshot, and an enlarged, now visible vein ran through the center of his forehead.

"They fear this emotion most. Fear is their greatest weakness. Because they fear, they cultivate self-hatred. It is a petty hatred, nothing more than hatred of themselves and everyone like them." Aloysius gripped the sides of the table with his powerful hands, and leaned forward, so his face was only two or three inches away from Jacob's. His muscles seemed to tense, and his voice rose. "They submerge this hatred for themselves and one another, and then they express it to those who are different from them. And you must understand, I am different from them. My anger is pure. That much I know. It is not tinged with hatred. But it is inexplicable. I am sometimes confused and consumed by it, and then consumed by this confusion." He let loose his hold on the table, and leaned back, though still remaining tense. Aloysius tapped his combat boots on the floor. His voice much calmer, though his rigid body gave clue to his emotions, he spoke again. "If the world could be a different place, without pain, without betrayal. You must understand, my pupil, I am angry because of the suffering."

"But what is the source of suffering?" asked Jacob, seated with Aloysius beneath the Bo-tree.

"Attachment is the source of suffering."

"What is the source of attachment?"

"Desire is the source of attachment."

"What is the source of desire?"

"Illusion is the source of desire."

"What is the source of illusion?"

"Desire is the source of illusion."

"What is the source of desire?"

"Attachment is the source of desire."

"What is the source of attachment?"

"Suffering is the source of attachment."

"O master, how is one to break free from this cycle of cause and effect?"

"Cultivate right learning and you will have the illusion of freedom."

"How does one shatter the illusion of freedom and achieve true freedom?"

"Does the feather shatter glass, my pupil?"

"No, master. Only the hammer shatters glass."

"And what force drives the hammer?"

"The hammer is driven by the willful soul."

"You must have surmised by now that the hammer is the body, and anger is the force behind the hammer."

"You have taught me much. I must apologize for my ignorance."

"And to you, pupil, I must apologize for all of the distractions."

"What do you mean?"

"My arms! My arms are thrashing about—I cannot control them."

"But master, your arms are perfectly still."

"What are *you* talking about? Can't you see that I'm trying to fly? I want more control! I must have more control!" They sat in apparent serenity beneath the Bo-tree, its leaves and branches still in the midst of a rising storm. Menacing thunderclouds passed overhead and the wind howled in anger. How long did they sit there, unable and unwilling to speak any more? For a period of time equal to the successive life spans of ten thousand Indras, or a single blink of Brahma's eye.

When they returned to the cafe, they once again were sitting across the table from one another, maintaining their silence. The murmur and gurgle of the crowd hurt Jacob's ears, and the stench of sweat and tobacco smoke began to grow unbearable. Sensing their meeting to be over, Jacob rose and turned to leave, and then caught his first sight of her. An exquisite, graceful beauty. She noticed Jacob too, and she delicately lifted a glass of white wine to her lips with her white porcelain hands.

"Jacob, come here tomorrow at noon. You will meet her then," announced Aloysius.

As Jacob walked past her, she acknowledged him with a smile, and he blushed.

Jacob slept uneasily that night, tossing, turning, indeed, engaging in a whole series of bed gymnastics. The source of his tribulations? He dreamed he was running through the corridors of Occult Sciences, and behind him, he heard Govind's voice, "No, no, no, no going in there!" Jacob ran into the hall of cubicles, and then stopped suddenly. For at the uppermost center cell, he saw her. The woman from the cafe. She stood with her long arms outstretched, beckoning him to her. Her long, ink black hair flowed magnificently over her bare white shoulders, and her perfectly smooth skin seemed to radiate a cool moonlight. She called his name, and after a "Yes, my love, I am coming!" Jacob began to climb a ladder to reach her. Hearing Govind wheezing and panting, he looked below him and beheld his naked, sweaty body near the foot of the ladder, though he seemed to moving with increasing speed. The portly doorman proved alarmingly agile: just as Jacob reached for the woman's outstretched hand, he felt Govind's chubby fingers straining for his feet. A second later, Govind pulled Jacob by the ankle, and with tremendous, superhuman strength, he flung him mercilessly from the ladder and into the darkness below. As he plummeted, he heard laughter—male or female he could not remember. He awoke before his body hit the ground.

In the morning, Jacob felt inexplicably angry. He screamed at Nicodemus, he cursed the NPR announcer for lagging with the weather report, and he threw two plates against the wall in punishment for daring to still be polluted with old, dried food particles. He sat on his living room couch—a dusty, lumpy brown thing which would have been flea infested were it not for Nicodemus's hairlessness—and tried to calm himself through the dual methods of cigarette smoking and counting backwards from fifty. (It was a difficult method, for the act of counting had to be separated from the act of smoking—to combine the two would have done nothing but lead to fifty quick inhalations of the smoke. The art lay in the separation, and it was the practice of such an art that peace could be found). When his anger finally found a cage in which to lock itself up somewhere not too deep in his unconscious, Jacob's mind was made free for obsession. Romantic obsession. Sexual obsession. He consciously conjured the image of the woman who had blessed him with a smile at the cafe. He remembered his dream from the night before, but concentrated only on the pleasant parts: her arms *were* outstretched to him; she *did* call his name—she even *knew* his name. "What is your name, my shimmering loveliness," he said aloud. "Angelica? Gabrielle?" What would she be like? How would she speak? A deep sultry voice or a sweet, melodious one? What would her long, luxurious hair smell like? Could he find refuge in its scent, sweetness in her touch, love in her eyes.....

Jacob had very little experience in romantic matters. It was true, he did have a certain charm that some women found appealing. It was his shyness that some found attractive. But it was not mere timorousness—it was the combination of his awkwardness and, when properly questioned about matters about which he cared, his youthful exuberance and seriousness of purpose. It was for this reason that he was able to move conversation beyond downcast eyes and a whispered, "Hello, how do you do." Yet, no potential romance had, as of yet, moved beyond initial attraction, for upon completing his final sentence on the topic that had moved him so, he would withdraw, not knowing what else to say, and afraid that he had offended by his enthusiasm. Whoever may have posed the question that captivated his interest and led to his effulgence would be startled by the hasty but neat folding up of his personality. Years upon years of living this way had made him outwardly pessimistic about love and its possibility, though it also, made him over-eager to see it where it might not be.

But this time would be different. Jacob would not let this woman pass by—he was to meet her. He had a reason to speak to her, something in common, and she wanted to meet him. How could he go wrong?

Jacob sat across the white marble top table from Aloysius and the beautiful woman who had already entered his dreams. Her name was Phoebe, Phoebe Kelli. Nervously rubbing the smooth marble with his fingers as he admired Phoebe's soft, pale skin, Jacob had said very little after Aloysius' introduction. The three sat with espresso cups set before them, like old friends simply enjoying the atmosphere of a relaxing cafe, needing to say little, and finding the enjoyment of one another's company as satisfying as conversation. Indeed, nothing could have been further from the truth. The three gathered together were hardly relaxed: Aloysius was always anxious no matter his demeanor, and Jacob was almost agitated enough to give up all romantic possibilities and run screaming from the cafe in a rush of uncontrollable nervous energy. Cafe Feu d'Amour was hardly a relaxing place for someone who had love on their mind. Everywhere one looked, paintings and sculptures proclaimed the beauty of love's physical expression. And Phoebe was waiting...waiting...waiting for someone to speak, to captivate her interest, to make her laugh, to pay her a compliment.

Aloysius at last rose to leave. "Have to go, Phebe. Behave yourself." She smiled, and exhaled cigarette smoke through her puckered lips.

"I really have to tell you—you are really rather beautiful," Jacob blurted out once Aloysius had walked out of earshot. Why he had spoken these words he would later never quite understand. It was perhaps something about the penetrating way that she looked at him which forced him to say what he was thinking. Or was it that the countless relief sculptures of medieval India's sexual athletes joined in a resounding chorus of "Tell her she's beautiful! Tell her she's beautiful!" casting a love spell on the earnest young man?

"Yes," she responded, unexpectedly and unembaressedly. Not coldly, but, really rather matter-of-factly. She smiled and waved to someone beyond Jacob. It must have been Aloysius, saying a final goodbye before leaving the cafe.

"I mean, I felt drawn to you," Jacob blundered on "as if I had to speak to you...Even before Aloysius told me that we would be meeting." And then he sat, saying nothing, embarrassed, but unable to take his eyes away from her.

Phoebe put out her cigarette, and uncrossed her legs. She pulled herself to the edge of her seat, and put both her hands flat on the tabletop. Jacob stared at her hands, wanting so desperately to touch them, to feel their softness.

"Jacob, do you know why you're here?" She said in a serious, controlled tone, measuring her words. Jacob remained mute, though she paused for a reply. Was the question rhetorical? What was he to say? The truth was unspeakable—in his mind, he was there on a first date.

"Let me tell you, then," she resumed. "Jacob, I take care of my body. I heed its desires, I satisfy its cravings, its hungers. When my body desires, I satisfy it. Nothing stands in the way of that, nothing, or no one. Do you understand?" Jacob nodded.

"That fulfillment is how I free myself from desire. The feminine body—" she stopped and she reached out to touch his hand with her fingertips, "the feminine body throughout history has been a tool of salvation. A tool, Jacob. It is now *my* tool. Sex, sex is everything to me." Jacob's heart pounded, and his armpits and palms began to perspire. "But also nothing. Meaningless."

There was nothing for him to say. She leaned towards him even closer and whispered, her moist, hot breath licking his ear lobe, and then trickling down the side of his neck, "So, that's enough of our lesson today—would you like to come up to my place for a drink?"

Shirt partially unbuttoned, shoes set neatly in the foyer, Jacob sat in Phoebe's living room on a rug-sized cushion. Absent was the traditional furniture arrangement of sofa and coffee table. "I prefer my party cushion," she told him. Phoebe and Jacob's first kiss had led to a tight hug and spirited half-roll across the soft pad. And then Phoebe excused herself, pushing away a flush and panting Jacob. Having regained his composure, he was now taking a cursory inspection of her place. A large hookah sat on each end of the cushion. Tantric mandalas were drawn in grey ash on the walls, and empty liquor bottles lay in the periphery of the cushion, along with several unemptied ashtrays. Phoebe walked in carrying a tray with two glasses of ice, a bottle of vodka, and a plate of hamburger meat. Liquor and meat—a thousand years ago it would have driven a brahmin mad to know of the transgressions of the tantrics. Nowadays, not so many cared. But tradition was tradition, so the contents of Phoebe's party platter was long ago ordained by her tantric forebears. She set the tray on the floor next to Jacob, and lit some jasmine-scented incense.

Sitting next to him, she scooped up a handful of ground beef and stuffed it into his mouth before he could answer her question, "Hamburger?" The pair drank a pint of vodka between them, and smoked three joints. It was now time for Phoebe to teach Jacob the lost arts of pleasure. Stoned, drunk, and with a belly-full of hamburger, Jacob was led to Phoebe's bedroom.

Their lovemaking reached the heights of perfection: Jacob was an apt pupil, eager to learn the ways of giving and receiving pleasure. After awhile, as Jacob shouted a loud "Ugh, ugh, aah,"—a coarse, amateurish orgasm—Phoebe uttered "Umm, my knee, put me, hummm. Ummm, my knee, pat me, hummmmmmmmm," in a low monotone, exhibiting the grace and control of an adept. Like Siva Nataraj calmly contemplating the wild dance of life expressed by his body, Phoebe mastered breath and voice even though her body convulsed in orgasm.

Exhausted, smiling beatifically, the two lay with their heads facing in opposite directions. She set her feet beneath his back, and he lay upon her folded legs. Bright rays of cosmic energy flowed from them, creating a three-foot thick, multi-directional aura. Yoni and linga only gently touched.

"To the East, Jacob!" Phoebe exclaimed, causing the golden aura to dissipate. "To the East! I've always turned to the East to find peace. To find knowledge. Knowledge and power." Jacob lifted his neck up, and stared down between his feet, where Phoebe's head lay. She looked to the ceiling as she spoke. "I should tell you something, though I think you must already know—I'm a bhairavi, a yogini...My yogic powers increase with every person I make love to..." Jacob dropped his head back onto his pillow. He had certainly felt a pang or two deep in his abdomen when they were wrapped around each other. Love? Maybe not. But something. Perhaps only the desire for it. She raised her head and smiled. "But I think you're different, Jacob. I know I hardly know you, but there's something special about you."

Those were words that Jacob had wanted to hear from lips as soft and sensuous as Phoebe's. He smiled, and drifted off into pink sunsetted alcoholic dreams, feeling her body's warmth while his remained in a narcotized, post-coital euphoria. As he slipped into a hangover in his sleep, Phoebe's presence made the pain bearable. When he awoke, she brought him three tablets of aspirin substitute and a bottle of natural spring water—she herself felt no ill after-effects. As

Jacob waited for the pain-relievers to drive his headache away,
Phoebe sat on the bedroom floor meditating. When she
awoke from her trance, Jacob knew it was time to leave. He
dressed, saying little or nothing. Before he left, Phoebe
handed him a small piece of paper with her telephone number
written on it.

Jacob came home thoroughly exhausted and still feeling
the effects of his hangover. When he opened his front door,
he was greeted by Nicodemus who jumped through the air
from atop a book shelf, landing on Jacob's shoulder. It was a
scolding; claws were dug into flesh in punishment for Jacob's
licentiousness. The cat was picked up by the folds of skin
behind its neck and dropped onto the ground by an
unregretful Jacob, who then stumbled across the cluttered
floor of his studio apartment, stripped down to his boxer
shorts, and got into bed.

But sleep didn't come. His mind was alive with images of
Phoebe. Phoebe laughing, smiling, kissing him, touching
him....Jacob had never made love to anyone before. He could
smell her perfume on himself; he could smell her body's
orgasmic ointments and sensual secretions that she had rubbed
and lathered all over his body. And Jacob ached while he
thought of her. He ached deep in his gut. His stomach
turned. He lost his now almost painful erection; turned over
on his side, bringing his knees to his stomach, and wrapped
his long thin arms around his pillow. Phoebe was more than
the physical presence with whom he had shared so much
pleasure just a short while ago. She was becoming the perfect
dream-vision which he had formed of her the night before.
She was softness and comfort, and why, she could even be—
there was always that chance—yes, she could be the fulfillment of Jacob's ancient desires for profound friendship and
unconditional acceptance. And with that thought, Jacob
drifted off into deep, dreamless sleep.

3.

"*Y*ou must understand something about temptation, Jacob. It is our way to flaunt the pleasures of the flesh before our very eyes, but only when we can resist its hold, when it cannot affect our spiritual core. When you are ready, you will find sex to be a powerful tool for your spiritual liberation, but you must guard yourself against mere lust. You have remained pure, have you not?" the Librarian asked Jacob, the very day after he had been with Phoebe.

Yes, my guru. I have," Jacob lied. How could he betray the intricate intimacies shown to him by Phoebe? He would serve his guru faithfully, but he would not break his heart with the news of he and Phoebe's lovemaking.

"Good. I feel that I have made an excellent choice with you. And what of the other...Aloysius?"

"I have met him, master. I sense his power—"

"His is a powerful way as well, but it is not for you. Resist his influence. He has gained much through his anger, but he will not progress to my level." Did Jacob hear the off-key tone of arrogance in his master's voice? "Learn from his discipline, Jacob, and learn from Phoebe the strength of concentration and singlemindedness."

Despite his denials to the Librarian, Jacob continued to visit Phoebe in her apartment in the next few weeks. Though after his first nervous phone call following their encounter, he was told never to go to the cafe to see her. He didn't ask her why, all too grateful that their lovemaking had meant as much to her as it did to him. Jacob had long fantasized about a lover, and Phoebe, in the weeks to come, was to satisfy the most urgent, even superficial aspect of that fantasy. But he so wanted to be in love—he wanted to tell her his secrets, to feel a faith that she would stay with him for the next day, and the next, to feel that he, with all his faults, was irreplaceable to her. He felt her distance from him. Jacob was not an especially emotionally controlled man, and indeed, his insecurities could lead to much emotional dependence, but he was a dreamer, and when his reality did not live up to his dreams, he would clear his throat, speak a few words, and make a few demands. He would of course shortly thereafter put on his coat, bow his head, and leave the site of conflict, but a minimal assertiveness was not entirely unknown to him.

Slightly disillusioned and wanting to be persuaded otherwise, he confronted Phoebe, ostensibly prepared to end their affair after only a few weeks. He wanted her to confide in him, to sit and talk to him for hours about the most mundane of things—now they only made passionate love, always accompanied by the tantric rites. He was special—she had told him so. But he could not stay in their relationship while she kept so much of herself hidden. When he said these things to her, Phoebe wept, and told him that she had never met any one like him before—that there was truly something "special" about him. That undefined word made many appearances in the conversations of their first few weeks together. She told him that she had been alone her entire life: her parents were peripatetic hippies that hustled her from ashram to ashram, never allowing her to stay anywhere long enough to make any friends. Jacob imagined an eight year old Phoebe, raven-locks even then flowing in the wind, desperately crying, holding on to the gates of a holy center, her merciless hippie parents trying to pull her away, while her helpless childhood friends bid her farewell.

Her parents never told her that they loved her, though they would unabashedly exclaim their love for their current guru, a particularly fragrant batch of patchouli, and of course, the Grateful Dead. Oh, she had heard her share of "Right on, Phoebe" and "Groovy, kid," but never "those words that a child so longs to hear," and which so many take for granted.

Jacob felt foolish for misreading her so, and Phoebe continued her tale of neglect and emotional want: She never learned what a good relationship could be. All her romances turned sour. Loneliness and fear made her distant. And then she wept. Jacob told her that he could understand what she went through. He hugged her. They sat in silence for a long while.

   And then Jacob told her his story. These were the heart-wrenching confessions that he so longed for, and now they were happening, and now he could share all the things that had gone into his making, and then, well, then, understanding would be achieved. He had always been dissatisfied with his life, a mundane middle-class upbringing if there ever was one. In college he could fill that emptiness within him—it was loneliness he knew—by learning new things, and feeling the power that came from that. He could imagine himself to be in different places, even as being different people. He chose to go to divinity school because he wanted to Know More, to know everything, he would tell people, and what better way than to study God. Sometime while he was there he had lost his faith. Not a faith in God, since he had never really had that, but faith in his ability to know, to learn what he truly wished to know. But what it was, what his true object was, he could not identify. It was a conflict that raged in his mind, he told her—he had lost his soul, he sometimes thought, lost it from skepticism, cynicism, and faithlessness. All that he had learned, instead of filling an emptiness, fed it, and made it grow.

   It was then that he found the Librarian. Did Jacob notice Phoebe's grimace at the mention of his name, or did he simply ignore it? The Librarian's own faith and power inspired him in a way that he had never been before. He renewed him, allowing Jacob to believe in things again. The Librarian seemed so free of hypocrisy, free of the tired ways and habits that Jacob felt to be so debilitating; in a word, he was pure. Of course, Jacob insisted, he didn't believe everything he was told –he was skeptical by nature– but he was willing to give it a try. Jacob's honesty to Phoebe reached its limits here. The truth was that his skepticism would always weaken and fade when in the old man's presence.

At last, confidences and life stories were exchanged between the lovers. Trust was established. Jacob's ego inflated to enormous proportions. He could now get on with being in love.

And he was in love. Their affair lasted two months, and followed a set pattern. Not necessarily a comfortable one, but unspoken rules, and one or two spoken ones, were set early on. Sex was always preceded by hamburger meat, and at least half a shot of vodka and a toke or two from a joint. This could not be changed, and Jacob never challenged it. He did look imploringly once, silently requesting that he be allowed to avoid at least the vodka since he was recovering from a cold, but Phoebe would not give in, no matter how much Jacob's soft, brown eyes pleaded. And Jacob was forbidden to speak to Aloysius. He never asked why, and simply assumed that he was dangerous—the Librarian had, after all, gave warning of him. To ensure that this code of silence was maintained, Jacob was not allowed to go to the Cafe Feu d'amour. Of course, these were small prices to pay for Phoebe's companionship and love. Rules were phrased as suggestions and requests, and relationship "agreements," so Jacob found them difficult to resist or question, were he ever so inclined.

But did it ever occur to him to ask why he was not allowed to call Phoebe past 7 pm? Or why they never went out at night? It did not. Perhaps he was desperate to keep what he had, but he never seemed so. Jacob trusted Phoebe. He loved her. And, indeed, whatever was to happen, whatever her intentions in initiating the affair, she loved him. At least...well...maybe she did.

What Jacob did have with Phoebe were afternoons. And what wonderful afternoons they were! Sensuous food, slippery, scintillating sex followed by profound discussions on Eastern Philosophy. They feasted on all-you-can-eat lunch specials at Chinese, Thai, Indian, Indonesian, and Japanese restaurants. They went for long, romantic walks in the park. And each day, without fail, they would return to Phoebe's apartment to fervently make love. It was difficult to say which Jacob enjoyed more—sex or conversation with Phoebe. Food almost always came in a distant second, except when the India-dome served greasy *dosas* and *Jaya Auntie's World Famous Sambar Delight*. (*Sambar*: it burned, it soothed, it lived again in the belching. It occupied three states of matter: solid before cooking, liquid when prepared, and finally after being taken into the body, it took a gaseous, nay, spirit afterlife). The day of the *sambar* special was perhaps the only time that both Phoebe and Jacob were reluctant to leave the site of their culinary pleasure for their diurnal quest for orgasm.

During his free nights, Jacob rested, thought of Phoebe, and read more and more about meditation and yoga, and practiced his morning lessons. He was far from an expert, his instruction had gone slowly, covering the basics. One thing was becoming clear to him: Jacob life had profoundly changed. He had found two teachers, one of whom was his lover and friend. Life became full, cynicism passed. Knowledge seemed graspable. Jacob had emerged from his isolation.

Yet, for all that was going well, Jacob was occasionally bothered by the lies he felt that he had to tell the Librarian. He knew that he would want to know of Phoebe, but Jacob could not reveal it. Jacob sensed that the relationship was to be a secret between Phoebe and himself, though she never said so. They were conspirators, accomplices, and the Librarian was not to know. But there were times when Jacob felt like he had to confess to his guru, to let him know of his great happiness, and promise to him that it would not change his desire to learn and practice the tantric way.

Seven weeks after Jacob and Phoebe's first day together, the Librarian said to Jacob, "Tell me again, Jacob, for I have forgotten." Jacob knew that his master forgot nothing, and only said so when he wished to test him. "Have you remained pure?" He had not asked that question since Jacob had first seen Phoebe. Jacob would lie again, difficult as it was. The first lie was born from fear of disapproval; this small untruth he had now was for the far more nobler purpose of serving to guard Love itself. Certainly the Librarian would understand such a thing.

"Yes, guru, I am still pure."

"Then I have chosen well."

Jacob continued to dream about Phoebe when he wasn't with her. It was always the same dream, the one he felt that brought her into his life. She stood in one of the cubicles, calling to him, calling his name, her arms outstretched. Jacob would try to control the events of the dream when he was half-awake, or still trying to drift off to sleep. But once he fell into deep sleep, the dream took its preordained course. Most of the time he would wake with a start after being flung into nothingness, but sometimes he would cease dreaming the remainder of the night, as if he had never ceased falling into the darkness. Jacob never mentioned his dream to her. "Why complicate matters?" he thought. And always, the next morning, he would wake up inexplicably tense, even angry, and would have to calm himself before his daily meeting with his guru. Jacob would not allow himself to become suspicious of Phoebe, whatever his dream-life might suggest, and pushed any doubts about her out of his mind.

On what turned out to be the last day of their affair, Jacob and Phoebe lay on her bed together with their backs leaning on the headboard, sharing a cigarette as they often would after making love.

"You've been visiting your librarian friend for quite awhile now....." Phoebe said unexpectedly. The couple rarely spoke about their shared affiliation with the Order. Jacob simply thought of Phoebe as another acolyte. Maybe she was more advanced in knowledge and more powerful than he right now, but he was certain that she was not held in as great favor.

"Yes, I have. But you've always known that Phoebe. Don't you meet with him for your lessons?" Jacob asked earnestly.

"With him? Ha! Used to, a long time ago. But he's got a new favorite now," she said bitterly.

"What do you mean?"

"No bullshit, Jacob. You know exactly what I mean. But you're a fool if you think his way can last. I've shown you what can be—just think what could happen if we got rid of his sedate mumblings and old-fashioned, half-witted monogamous nonsense and really put some life into the tantric way!"

"What are you talking about Phoebe?"

"He's been doing things his way for a long, long time," she continued. "You know, he's almost a hundred years old. An old, old man, not used to change," she said so disdainfully as to make Jacob nervous. He checked his watch. He usually left about an hour earlier, but Phoebe insisted that he stay a little while longer. She had ways of making such a request impossible to refuse. Besides, it was already a day of unusual requests, as the Librarian had asked to see him that evening instead of their usual morning meeting time.

"It's getting late Phoebe—I don't know what's gotten into you."

""Look at you—you're his subservient little *chamcha*. There are going to be some changes—pick a side!"

Jacob didn't understand what Phoebe was saying, thinking maybe that she was drunk, though she never got that way from the ceremonial vodka shot (or two) that they always took. Phoebe had held on to their cigarette as she became more agitated. Jacob pinched some more tobacco and rolled another one. He smoked, and thought of calm blue skies, and of softly falling snowflakes, just as his guru had told him to do in times of potential emotional unbalance. (It wouldn't work in another couple of minutes).

"Did I ever tell you that I made love to a man in a cemetery..." Phoebe said wickedly. "On a bed of human skulls. There's a lot of power in that...." Phoebe's manner had changed—her confession seemed to make her colder, more distant than she had ever been from Jacob. Perhaps it was the way she said the word power. But Jacob said nothing, and listened attentively, ever the sensitive lover.

"Shit! Did you hear that! What time is it?" she asked and turned to the clock-radio to see. "Oh, shit, it's 7:30! He'll kill you if he finds you here! Unless..." she looked Jacob over. "No way. He'll annihilate you!" Jacob jumped out of the bed and searched for the clothes he and Phoebe had so heedlessly thrown to the floor just a few hours before. He began to put on whatever items of clothing he could find, panicking as he recognized the voice coming from the living room. "Phoebe? You in there? Who're you talking to?" It was Aloysius.

Phoebe had arisen with Jacob, found his pants and handed them to him. "He'll rip your limbs off, tear your heart out of your chest and drink your blood. You better get out of here!" Jacob clumsily kissed an unreceptive Phoebe on the cheek, climbed out of the window onto the fire escape, and took thirty-seconds to put on the remainder of his clothing. He saw Aloysius fling Phoebe's bedroom door open, and then he tumbled down the thin metal steps.

Jacob walked along the bustling street on his way to the Library. The twilight brought a strange serenity to his troubled mind, bringing confidence that some explanation could be found for Phoebe's behavior and Aloysius's unexpected arrival. He would keep his faith in Phoebe. Twilight slowly faded to darkness. He became enchanted with the accreted, contradictory layers of the city, from the juxtaposition of hundred year old brick apartment buildings and gleaming, towering office buildings, to the sounds of English in its manifold urban manifestations. "Things always change," he surmised absentmindedly. They twist, degenerate, regenerate and grow into unidentifiable forms. They die and are reborn.

"Jacob, I need you."

"But, master, what can I, your humble servant do for you?" Jacob sat with his guru on the small rug in the Librarian's chamber.

"I've been preparing you. You have learned your lessons well—though Jacob, it is not in books that truth may be found. And you have resisted the temptations of Aloysius and Phoebe. You have not chosen their way. The book has chosen well. Now it is time for me to achieve my liberation. And you must help me."

"I am not so certain that I have resisted temptation..." Jacob said sorrowfully.

"Yes, you have, Jacob. You have seen the path of anger and you have resisted it. And you have yet to engage in the pleasures of the flesh."

"That is true," Jacob lied for the third time. But he bowed his head and looked down to the floor.

"Jacob? What's the matter?"

Jacob paused, and looked up, staring intently into the deep grey eyes of his teacher. He had learned so much from him, that small, ever serene man, who asked precious so little for his gifts of knowledge. "It's true," he said finally. "I've met the two, but, master, I've, I've..."

"Jacob. Tell me....you've been with her, haven't you?"

Jacob admitted everything: No, it meant nothing. Well, not nothing. O.K., O.K. I'm in love with her! Didn't mention it before, didn't think it was important. I know, I know, you told me I was chosen. Is that why you asked me if I was a virgin? He told him how it all began, all the odd arrangements, all the wonderful moments of life-giving passion and love, and, the apparent end, only two hours ago, with an inglorious escape through the bedroom window. And he told him how he was going to believe in her, for an explanation would be found.

"Jacob, you disappointed me. You may have just ruined everything." The old man had listened to Jacob's tale, not sympathetically, but with increasing disappointment. Another long, heavy silence settled before he spoke again. "I have been preparing you for something very important. You have spilled your seed for no true purpose. Pleasure, only pure pleasure— and with *her*! Didn't I warn you?"

"I would do anything to help you, you know that," Jacob pleaded. "I have the deepest respect for you and your teachings."

"I don't know. I've worked so hard to prepare you for this moment And now is the right time. Let us try, Jacob. Maybe you can still help me...We'll call your affair a purification rite, pudenda worship or something. Come on, help me with this." Jacob and his guru opened up volume upon volume of books and placed them on the floor. "Now hold on one minute" said the Librarian, and disappeared behind one of the bookstacks. He emerged a few minutes later, dressed in a black-lace teddy.

"It's my turn now Jacob. I need you."

"But guru, what is it that you want of me?" Jacob said, though he knew. He knew.

"Jacob, you must help me—it is time to overturn our rules, to grasp temptation and pleasure and force them to release the power of the kundalini. Enough talking, Jacob, I have prepared you for two months—you must help me now!"

Jacob assented. It was the least he could do to repay his guru for his kindness, even to make up for his own weaknesses of the flesh. And perhaps the Librarian would forgive him, and accept he and Phoebe's love.

But the time for such calculation was over: hands slid, fingers touched, one set at first apprehensively, and then both equally aggressively. Soon two pairs of legs entwined, and two tongues licked and tasted. The older man was thin and fit, and exhibited a true yogi's flexibility. Jacob had yet to learn the higher level asanas, though he surprised his teacher with many contortions learned from Phoebe.

"*Om Klim Strim,*" the Librarian began to chant, pronouncing each syllable slowly and carefully, as they grappled with one another. After at least an hour of their complicated maneuverings, the Librarian shouted out, "Oh, oh, oh, I've done it! Yes! Yes! I've done it! Oh, Jacob, don't you see, I've released the powers of my shakti. I've achieved liberation at last. Oh gods above and below! I am at one with the cosmic principle. Liberation through the abject. Thank you, Jacob, thank you."

They hovered together on the 72nd astral plane, observing the world below them. The Librarian had shed his body, it seemed to Jacob, though he still retained a familiar shape.

"I can tell that it's you, but there's something different about you—"

"You are seeing my soul-body. You recognize me because my earthly body is familiar to you. Same shape, different conditioning..." the Librarian answered as he spun himself around a full three hundred sixty degrees. "My soul-body is of course much less flabby than my earthly body. A flabby body is embarrassing enough, but a flabby unmuscular soul? A shame!"

Jacob looked at himself, and saw the flesh of his soul body ooze and undulate.

"Discipline!" the guru declared. "It takes discipline. You have a flaccid soul! Absolutely fluid, and porous. So easily influenced. Come with me, you're young. There's still time."

They saw such wonders. They somersaulted through galaxies. A troop of six identical Buddhas waved enthusiastically as they waltzed around Neptune. A meditating monk passing from the 72nd to the 73rd astral plane frowned on their frolicking They soared ever higher and faster towards a bright sun. As they began to penetrate the fiery orb, Jacob felt as if he were falling...and then he loss consciousness.

He awoke with his thumb stuck in his mouth, lying naked atop a makeshift bed of open books, and holding the cold, lifeless hand of the Librarian. Jacob's body tingled, and his toes and fingers wiggled of their own accord. He was reborn into a new world and nothing would be the same again. He heard the voices of Aloysius and Phoebe from down the corridor.

Book 2

4.

a deep thumping bass drove the hot, writhing bodies to the rhythmic beat. Dark, bared midriffs undulated calling forth primitive urges. Open hands were aggressively thrust above heads, and drops of sweat flew through the thick, humid air. Lights flashed in the dark night, revealing swaying and gyrating hips. The scents of the tribe filled the air, divulging allegiances: Calvin Klein, Estee Lauder, Obsession.

Joyous shouts provided a staccato accompaniment to the full throttle techno-bhangra sounds spun by D.J. Rasta Rajie the Bhangra Pakie. Jacob found himself pushed and pulled in this swirling mass of bodies, still in shock from his evening experiences with the Librarian. Phoebe and Aloysius had found him lying in fetal position next to the cold corpse of their mentor. Quickly surmising what had occurred—their leader's predilections were no great secret—they bowed their heads in obligatory mourning for a quick moment, and then whisked Jacob away while he declared, quite petulantly and ungratefully, Phoebe would later point out, "I'm still naked!" They clothed him while in Aloysius's jet black Lexus, after stopping by his place so Phoebe could make a quick phone call, and find something suitable for Jacob to wear, though she managed only to find a black t-shirt and ill-fitting blue jeans. She also brought a thermos of champagne and orange juice, which Jacob was ordered to chug-a-lug. "You need your Vitamin C," Phoebe said, feigning maternal concern. He could barely hear Aloysius murmuring, "Mother-fucker....goddamn motherfucker." And then, as far as Jacob could remember, they ended up here, wherever here was. His head reeled for a good two minutes every ten—perhaps the

Mimosas were drugged? Bhangra is the word he heard, trying to figure out where he was. Bhangra with a breathy b-h.

They sat on the second level at a table overlooking the dance floor. Well dressed young men shivered and shook in front of long, luscious-haired beauties, who produced sonic booms with each hip shake. Mild-mannered software engineers became hip-swaying, pelvis thrusting maniacs, their glasses fogged up by the sight of near-naked coeds (all virgins of course) bouncing their ample breasts up and down. Two Nusrat Fateh Ali Khan look-alikes, surrounded by their groupies took stock of each other from across the dance floor, looking for a chance to hybridize sumo wrestling and kawwali wailing. Alas they would never meet under the flashing lights, though their presence sparked rumors throughout the club that one of them was the real McCoy, and was in town to sign a contract to replace Eddie Vedder as lead singer of Pearl Jam.

The music softened for the D.J., whose voice boomed in an affected West Indian accent, "A shout to the Indian posse in the House tonight. From Trinidad, from East Africa, from England, from Fiji, and those of you from the homeland. We're here to keep you dancing through the diaspora."

Before he fell into another dizzy spell, Jacob overheard two women remark, "Can you believe that accent?" "I know—he does it every time. You know he's from New Jersey."

Jacob finally interrupted his long, mesmerized stare at the dance floor, and looked up, expecting to see Phoebe and Aloysius, but they had left. He looked back down to the floor, and thought he could see her lean figure making its way through the crowd. For no good reason, Jacob thought that perhaps he should get a drink. It was, after all, what one did to pass the time in a night club. But money? He reached in his pocket, and pulled out a twenty, placed there no doubt by an ever-thoughtful Phoebe. He headed for the bar.

A mild mannered doctoral candidate in Sanskrit Studies at the internationally renowned Institute of Oriental Studies, which was attached to a nearby prestigious university, saw the vacancy created by Jacob and quickly took a seat. He had been elbowed, poked, pushed and sweated upon by far too many people that night, and now looked forward to a respite at this table before leaving this bhangra business behind. He had come on a whim, feeling guilty after a confrontation with one of his hot-headed undergraduates. "You wouldn't know a real Indian if you saw one!" the young man shouted at him. Yes, shouted! "You're trying to freeze us in time to satisfy some silly fantasy of yours! You're nothing but an Orientalist!" That was no way to speak to a future internationally famous Sanskritist. Ephraim Stockwell had his revenge. He gave the student a C minus in his course. That little Sodomite post-structuralist firebrand would not be studying Sanskrit anytime soon. Now, of course he was an Orientalist, but what was wrong with that? Anyway, here he was, away from his books and his beloved Sanskrit poetry, getting to know "real" Indians.

Leaning on it for support, Jacob looked down the length of the bar, and watched as gold and platinum cards were placed down in rapid succession with a loud "thwack" by square-jawed muscle men wanting to impress. The intended audience for these displays of financial credibility were the three highly efficient, though thoroughly disinterested women standing behind the bar. The first bartender stood to the far left, pouring vodka, wearing a tight black jumper, black lipstick, and kept her black hair cut military style. To her left, a pale skinned platinum blonde popped open seven bottles of ice-cold beer, sending bottle caps flying through the air. And closest to Jacob, a blonde in a pink mini-skirt and pink halter-top jiggled from head to toe as she blended a syrupy concoction in a mixer. His head spun for a moment. Trying to regain his full consciousness, he focused on the conversation of the club-goers next to him.

"That one over yonder I call licorice stick," a man said with a Texas drawl. "And the one in the middle—she's pepper-mint stick. And here, this one, our bartender, I call Piggly Wiggly. And I'll tell ya'll a little secret—if you touch her on her little belly button, Piggly Wiggly gets giggly!"

After a brief burst of laughter, Jacob sensed tensions rise when a voice asked quite seriously, "Don't you think that's demeaning to women?"

Jacob felt a slight shiver of excitement when he heard the strength and resolution in the young woman's voice. He turned to look at her, while she stared intensely at her misguided friend.

"Come on, Sunita, I'm only kidding."

"O.K. Tex. But watch yourself."

Tex, alias Anil Chadha, responded with a wide, obsequious grin. Discussing "women," not "gals," with Sunita always left him unsure of himself, and he needed his self-esteem for the contest tonight. He was a rising champion of the Bhangra Bull-Riders circuit—a nationwide touring competition in search of the best of all mechanical bull-riders of sub-continental descent. He earned his living now from prize money and his salary as a sales clerk at a country-western clothing boutique. Some say that the secret of his bull-riding success was in his get-up: his well-polished, shiny eel boots, his Wrangler blue-jeans, his mango-sized belt buckle with his name emblazoned upon it, and his palomino colored Western shirt and bolo tie. But those in the know attributed Anil's achievements to something in the air in his hometown of Lubbock, Texas that had made its way into the Chadha blood, leading to a hunger for success and a love of competition. He had long competed on the mainstream mechanical bull-riding circuit in Texas, but he had grown tired of performing for all-white audiences. Now he had a chance to show his skills to his own people, finding resolution to his own personal case of diasporic schizophrenia. Anil's brother Sunil was also a great success, though in the far less glamorous field of ayurvedic urine therapy. Sunil had discovered his own way to join together East and West by marketing the therapy through self-help seminars at community colleges all across Texas, from "Big Bend to Beaumont," as his prize-winning brochure declared.

Sunita let Tex's transgression pass. She had learned to be more careful in choosing her battles. Ever a foe of Indian patriarchy in all its forms, from marriage arrangement to the casual sexism of her male Indian friends, she had painfully learned that it was not worth her effort to educate Tex. She chalked up his gender insensitivities to culture—he was a Texan after all. But she did like him, and she knew that he was only trying to be funny. Besides, she was already annoyed by all this silly, macho bhangra bull-riding, and didn't want to aggravate herself anymore.

Jacob felt an overwhelming desire to meet the young Indian woman, but was not sure why. He certainly did not have seduction in mind, and anyway he was hardly practiced in its art to attempt it now. He introduced himself rather awkwardly, expecting a quick rebuff. He had comforted himself in advance with the thought that the humiliation of her expected rejection would last only until his next dizzy spell. But Sunita took hold of his outstretched hand and shook it, much to the surprise of Tex, and Vikram, who was technically on a date with her.

Why had she taken this stranger's hand? It was a harmless gesture of goodwill, but her reasons went perhaps a little deeper. Jacob had reminded her of someone in his awkward- ness and evident shyness, which was an accurate appraisal of Jacob's personality in general, though Sunita may only have been reading Jacob's drug-induced haze as reticence. She introduced Tex, and Jacob was a little startled by the strange outfit of the tall, lanky young man. A handsome, suspicious Vikram, in turn, flexed his prodigious shoulder and neck muscles, and then finally reached out and firmly shook Jacob's hand.

"Have you ever seen this many Indians in one place?" Tex goodnaturedly asked, engaging Jacob in light conversation.

"Thank you, Tex," Sunita said to herself. She didn't know what to say to Jacob, though she wanted to hear him speak. He had disturbed something in her, and made her remember in a way she had not let herself do in what seemed a long time.

Jacob was only mildly interested in Tex's conversation, though he found Tex's brief History of Bhangra, in which he traced its folk origins in the Punjab and discussed its contemporary flowering as a modern, urban dance music in all the major cities, from London to Chicago, to be quite instructive. As he listened to Tex, Jacob could not help staring at Sunita. He had first been impressed by the deference paid to her by Tex, which could quickly be sensed. Now he realized that she was physically beautiful too, resembling the impossibly idealized temple sculptures of South India with her large-bust, well-rounded hips and thin waist. But she had come to life with far more realistic proportions. She was not too top-heavy to stand upright, which must surely have been the case for the models posing for those ancient, lusty sculptors. Her statuesque form was animated by her expressive, intelligent eyes, graced by long black eyelashes, her soft, chocolate brown skin, and her long, lush, black hair. She wore black pants that began a stylish flare at the bottom of her calves, and an unbuttoned, almost transparent cream-colored shirt that flowed over a tight, cleavage-exposing black bodice.

Sunita's interest in Jacob, though generally well-hidden by her demeanor, did in fact manifest itself despite her best efforts to the contrary. The collected force of psychic and somatic interest –it was "interest" wasn't it– focused in her nipples, which now stood up at rigid, fully erect attention. Yes, her blinkers were on, and Jacob's eyes were fixed on them.

"Hey, man, what the hell do you think you're doing! You're ogling my girlfriend. there!"

"I am not your girlfriend, Vikram Kapur!"

"Hey, Sunita, what are you talking about, huh? I'm a liberal and all, but look, I'm into monogamy! One woman, one man!"

"Vikram, this our third date...Third!" She waved three fingers dangerously close to Vikram's eyes. "And probably our last!" Sunita turned and walked away, obediently followed by Tex, who thought it wise to take Sunita's side when she fought with Vikram, which occurred once a week for as long as she had known him, almost ten years. Despite this record, they had decided a few before to explore a romantic dimension to their longstanding friendship.

Sunita had quite unfairly turned on him, Vikram thought, so he now turned on Jacob, the one responsible for ruining his date. "What the hell do you think you're doing here, anyway, man? Following around and looking at our women like that?"

Vikram expected an answer, but he did not get one. Jacob's dizzy spells struck again, but this time with far greater effect. Perhaps it was Sunita, or maybe it was the threat of a sound beating from Vikram. Whatever the cause of Jacob's intensified reaction to the spiked mimosas, he swooned just as the question-mark in Vikram's inquiry rounded the corner and began its downward journey. Just as Jacob hit the floor, the six-five, three hundred pound bouncer Dirk, whose sole thought through the evening had been, "If only these people ate red meat," made his way to pick up the unconscious body. He would search for friends or next of kin in the immediate vicinity, and if this proved fruitless, he would deposit it into the club office. Not the street, as Dirk would have wanted, since the club's owner feared lawsuits far more than a little vomit on his vinyl-covered couch. Poor Dirk would have to sit by this one if he couldn't find anyone to take him home. And he found no one, as Vikram quickly disappeared when out of the corner of his eye he saw the glasses on the bar jump with each of Dirk's approaching steps.

"Try your luck astride the great bull Zam-Zammah!" a voice called enthusiastically over the p.a. system on the second dance floor. "He who ride Zam-Zammah the longest will hold the Punjab! Who will be first?"

Tex was still in a state of shock. He was only second runner-up; the highest two honors were now to be contested by the two Nusrat Fateh Ali Khan lookalikes.

"Look at them up there...No form, no poise...All that training down the tubes," Tex sullenly complained to Sunita.

Nusrat Fateh Ali Khan number one had just mastered his pacing, and was signalling for increased speed when the music suddenly stopped. Power was cut off to the bull, catching it in mid-leap. At first one hysteric, horrified shriek could be heard from the next room. And then three sharp bursts. The lights in the entire club were thrown on. A chorus of primal screams erupted, and then silence. Bhangra patrons stood staring at each other, uncertain what to do.

The emcee announced authoritatively, "Contest is indefinitely postponed due to circumstances beyond our control. We will hold a rematch."

"Excellent!" shouted Tex. Sunita glared icily at him. He stopped smiling.

"Is there a doctor on the premises?" the emcee continued. "All other persons are asked to please leave the club and go home, except for trained medical personnel. Those persons please report to the main dance floor. We need some room in here. Everyone please go home."

A group of twenty five earnest looking bespectacled young men and women –all medical students or residents qualifying as "trained medical personnel"– headed for the main dance floor from the Bhangra Bull-riding room.

"Great crowd control at a bhangra—asking for a doctor!" Tex joked to an unresponsive Sunita.

Jacob was tending cows, gently guiding them through luxuriant green grass to a lazy, deep blue river. There he witnessed an exquisite sight. A soft blue-skinned Phoebe was bathing in the water near to the banks, her loose silk sari tucked up between her legs, and her voluptuous bare breasts radiating a divine light. Jacob's mouth watered. Phoebe turned to her devotee and split herself into a thousand identical Phoebes—a female Krishna with a single male cowherd. Jacob, however was not up to the task. Male fantasy can be so cruel. He began to sweat nervously, and the words "I can't" were caught in his throat. He woke with a start.

"What are you saying, little man?"

Jacob looked up to a pockmarked face wrongly proportioned: a large red mouth full of yellowed teeth where eyes should have been, and two beady eyes took the place of a normally positioned human mouth. An upside down pug-nose flared with each wheezy breath of the oversized face. Jacob stayed still, his muscles remaining tense from his nightmare. But was this ugly face part of the dream? Had he woken up? He winced as drops of tepid, greasy sweat landed on his face. He was awake.

"What's the matter, huh? You were lying there saying – what was it– 'eeeii-crrooouow.' What's that mean? Do you speak their language or something?" The face disappeared and then Jacob heard a deep, gravelly laugh. He rolled his eyes upwards and saw that the face was connected to a head, bald though it was, and the head to a thick neck, and the neck to a massive torso. He couldn't see any legs without overextending his own neck, though he was certain that the two bowling balls he sensed to be just behind his ears were probably the gargantua's knees.

"Yup. 'Eeeeii-crrooouow.' What happened to you anyway? A little jungle-fever or something? I saw you standing there and just all of a sudden collapse. You were pretty easy to find in that crowd." More uncontrollable laughter. "Well, now that you've come to, it's about time that you get out of here. Let's go, get up."

"I-I-can't move," Jacob said worriedly.

"Are you drunk or something?"

"No, not drunk. I just can't move."

It was at that moment that the comfortable rumble of the music stopped, and Dirk and Jacob heard the chorus of blood-curdling screams.

"I better see what's going on out there!" said Dirk excit-edly, and rushed, as well as he could, out the door.

Now attracting more attention that he perhaps ever had before, Ephraim Stockwell was in no state to respond to all of the eyes trained upon him. He was now wearing an additional item of clothing—a finely crafted yellow silk scarf tightly fastened around his neck. Tight enough to strangle him. He was, or more correctly, his corpse, was the cause of the numer-ous shrieks in the club, not to mention the termination of this particular bhangra. Just a few minutes before, someone had nudged him upwards, thinking he was drunk as he lay slumped over his table. The spectacle of his bulging eyes and bleeding tongue –he had bit it as he gasped for air– was quite enough to scare the revelers around him. The call for medical attention was for the sake of propriety. He was clearly already dead when discovered.

Outside the club, the bhangra patrons milled about confusedly, hailing taxi cabs, waiting in line for pay phones, or fetching their elegant yet practical vehicles. News of the dead body and probable murder (suicide was quickly ruled out by Piggly Wiggly, though a formal coroner's report had yet to be filed) had already made its way out to the crowd, and set off a buzz of speculation and rumor. Some said it had to be gang-related, while others insisted that it was all probably a publicity stunt by D.J. Rasta Rajie.

Nusrat Fateh Ali Khan number two was heard to insist that the murder was an attempt to cheat him of his Bhangra Bull-riding crown, though he became visibly nervous when asked, "Do you really think that someone would kill another human being for the crown, especially when it isn't even the National Championships?" Khan number two responded by suggesting that the body probably wasn't real anyway, and that such a hoax would certainly not be beyond his competitors. Tex, with Sunita at his side, had the bad luck of nudging his way past the Khan number two circle, gaining stares and knowing nods.

Elsewhere in the crowd, two or three enterprising youths, advertising their own bhangra parties, promised later hours, more dancing and a murder-free environment. Taxi cabs lined up along the curb, but the arrival of the police squad cars and ambulance forced them to try and park elsewhere, though the crowd now spilled out into the street, making it difficult to maneuver. Horns blared, curses in Hindi and English were shouted, and police officers shined flashlights and swaggered. The party was over.

One of the bared midriff co-eds ran up to her friends and frantically warned, within earshot of Sunita and Tex, "There's a carload of Aunties out there! We better get out of here!" She was not referring to just any group of Indian aunties,

though the sudden presence of even the run-of-the-mill
variety might have struck fear into the hearts of these young
women just discovering their sexuality away from the watchful
eyes of their parents. She was, in fact, speaking of that group
of middle-aged Indo-American women who had formally
organized and taken to terrorizing the younger members of
the bhangra scene. The Aunties as an organization was started
by a group of concerned mothers who discovered that their
young daughters had given up their chastity while away in
college. They made it their sworn duty to never allow such a
thing to occur again in the Indian community. To fulfill that
solemn oath, they would file a report to a young unmarried
woman's parents whenever she dared to bare her midriff, or for
that matter, smoke a cigarette in public. Along with a full
report of the infraction, the Aunties provided their own
recommendation for disciplinary action, which invariably was
to send the hapless misfit back to India for re-indoctrination
and arranged marriage.

Sunita and Tex pushed their way to the fringe of the
crowd.

"So, Sunita, should we wait for Vikram?"

"Ah, Tex, he drives me crazy sometimes with his macho
garbage. You know, I think he probably already left....Hey,
Tex, look over there." Sunita pointed to a curious sight in the
alley way on the side of the club. A large, hulking mass,
carrying a much smaller body, was clearly attempting to hide
himself and his load as he tiptoed through the alleyway,
clinging to the side of the building. He seemed unaware of
the absurdity of his trying to appear inconspicuous, though
the mass, known as Dirk when outside of dark alleyways, was
only following orders. "Get rid of that shithead in my office
before I have even more headaches with the cops! And don't
let anyone see you!" he was told. The shithead in question was
none other than Jacob, and now he found himself alone,
deposited in an alleyway, with Dirk's final words before he ran
off —"Later, sucker" still in his mind.

"Isn't that the guy I was talking to before? The one
Vikram went apeshit on," Sunita said as she walked toward

Jacob, with Tex following closely behind. "What was his name?"

"Jason...no, Jack.....Jacob. His name was Jacob," responded Tex.

"That's right. Jacob. Well, Jacob, what are you doing here?" she said, now standing in front of him.

Jacob looked up to Sunita and felt a tingle from the top of his toes to the tips of his fingers. That electric charge must have energized his muscles, allowing him to slowly rise to answer her. He was in control of his body again, at least for the moment. He stood up and leaned against the brick wall.

"I'm not really sure what happened. I must have passed out...That bouncer brought me out here. There was some trouble in the club and they wanted to get rid of me. I think someone put something in my drink." Jacob was trying to find an explanation. In the back of his mind, he knew it must have been Phoebe who drugged him, but he was not ready to face that possibility.

"Well, can you walk?" asked Sunita, concerned.

"I think so." He tried walking, but tottered and then reached out to support himself by taking hold of Sunita's wrist. She put his arm around her neck, and the three of them walked out of the alleyway.

"Did you come with someone? Should we get you a cab?" Sunita asked.

"I think they left me here. A cab is fine." He looked at Sunita. He didn't know it, but it was a pleading look. He desperately wanted her sympathy and help. "I mean, I'm sure I'll be O.K."

"Look, you can come home with us."

"Sunita!!" rebuked Tex. He had seen the invitation coming, but had hoped that she would have better sense. "Can we talk?"

They left Jacob leaning against the wall, and took a few steps away.

"What do you think you're doing?" Tex fiercely whispered. "You don't even know him! And what's this 'us' crap. I was going home to my place."

"Come on, Tex, he needs our help. I've got a good feeling about him. We're just giving him a place to crash. And besides, you're going to be there to protect me," she coaxed, and then fluttered her long black eyelashes.

"Yeah, right. It's more like you'll end up protecting me."

"Thanks!" she started to turn toward Jacob.

"So, you'll give this guy a break, but you won't give a break to Vikram!" Sunita ignored Tex, and walked back to Jacob.

"It's settled. You can come home with us." Jacob looked at her gratefully, and mustered his strength to walk on his own. As they left the alley and passed the crowd in front of the club, Jacob felt another dizzy spell, and leaned on Sunita. She put her arm around his back to support him.

"Sooooo-nita! Sooooo-nita Chidh-amb-aram! Is that you?" Sunita turned to see one of the Aunties in uniform, a bright fuchsia salwar-kamiz.

"Oh, hi, Nachu Auntie." She dropped her hand from Jacob's back and smiled uncomfortably. "How are you doing? It's such a pleasure to see you!"

"Yes, it is quite a surprise, Sunita. Quite a surprise! Do Mummy and Daddy know you're here?" Padma sucked her teeth and shook her head. "It doesn't look that way. I'm afraid I'm going to have to report you." The militant Auntie strode off, leaving Sunita angry at herself that she could still be intimidated, even now that she was twenty-five years old.

"You carry him, Tex," she growled.

They walked down the block and waited at the curb for a taxi cab. A black Lexus screeched to a stop next to the threesome. The tinted front window rolled downward. "Jacob?" It was Phoebe. Puzzled, she squinted her eyes and furrowed her brow. And then the car sped away, leaving Tex, Sunita and Jacob to reflect upon the meaning of that strange encounter.

5.

Ín the morning, Tex shuffled out the front door, awakening Jacob. Still groggy, Jacob tried to piece together the events of the night before. He remembered suffering from dizzy spells on the cab ride home. And then a vague memory of the driver resurfaced: angry at having to stop and wait at a convenience store while Tex stood in line to buy chewing tobacco, the cabbie shouted to Sunita, "Miss, I've killed six people in Islamabad! Six People! I'm losing my patience with this cowboy friend of yours!" After arriving at Sunita's apartment, Jacob was taken to the couch, and groggily watched as Tex accompanied Sunita to her bedroom, telling her that he was doing his duty as her friend. Jacob remembered barely hearing a heated argument conducted in whispers. And then he heard the sounds of furniture being moved in front of the bedroom door. He fell asleep soon afterwards.

Here he was, in a beautiful stranger's apartment, glad he was there though embarrassed by the circumstances. He was comforted by the lingering scent of jasmine incense. The cozy, overstuffed couch he was lying upon was much softer than his own. Allowing his eyes to roam the room, he took note of the sofa chair and coffee table with magazines strewn upon it, the only sign of disorder in the well-kept room. He fixed his eyes on the bronze Shiva Natraj on the bookshelf. The living room windows were open, and a fresh breeze blew in, bringing a smile to his face. Sunita emerged from her bedroom, dressed in blue jeans, and a short-sleeved, cropped sweater that tantalizingly suggested that a glimpse of her navel might be had. He looked at the slight thigh-level tear on her jeans, and then up to her eyes. She smiled, said she would make some coffee, and then pulled open the window blinds, allowing in bright morning sunshine.

Having gratefully accepted Sunita's offer to use her shower, Jacob stepped into her bedroom, which he had to pass through to get to the bathroom. Jacob noticed two framed photographs set on the dresser drawer just inside the door, and turned to examine them. Sunita's father was a man of medium height, with thinning, greying hair. He carried a dignified paunch. Her mother was a thin woman. She kept her hair up—he couldn't tell if it was as long as Sunita's. Sunita had taken her father's bright eyes, and her mother's lips. What else had she inherited from them? He wondered what they were like—were they stern? were they loving? Where did Sunita get her already apparent self-assurance? What tragedies and traumas and experiences of warmth and love did they share in their collective family memories? Jacob looked at the other photo, which portrayed Sunita and her sister, who seemed a few years younger than her. How easy it was to see the pride with which these young women had comforts and small luxuries lavished upon them. The sisters had the same mischievous, almost conspiratorial smile. What secrets had they shared with one another and excluded these two others so apparently close to them?

Jacob turned from the photographs and walked to the slightly opened window. A scarf with Indian design was laid along the window sill. A light breeze blew in, causing the scarf to ripple and flutter, but it was kept on the sill by a few sea shells and a couple of stones. He looked over his shoulder to Sunita's bed which she had left unmade, with covers thrown open. "Where did Tex sleep?" he wondered.

Not wanting to take advantage of Sunita's hospitality by being excessively nosy, Jacob ended his brief inspection of her room, and walked around the bed and into the bathroom. He took a shower. Whatever drug had affected him the night before had worked its way through his system, finally leaving him sober and rational again. After dressing himself, Jacob joined Sunita on the couch, where a mug of coffee and a bagel had been set out for him. The television was on, but its volume was turned off. She was monitoring it for news of the murder at the bhangra. Jacob felt a little foolish in Aloysius's clothes, which were too big for him, and which still retained the nightclub smell of stale smoke and spilled alcohol. In the next hour or so that Tex was gone searching for a newspaper, Jacob was to learn a great deal about Sunita over what he surmised to be a pot of Sulawesi-Kalusi, brewed to a dark hue and a robustly spicy nut, yet fruity flavor.

He sensed a deep sadness about her when they first met the night before. Maybe it was the way she kept silent, or the way she looked at him, wanting to speak, but choosing to listen instead. But now, it was not difficult for Jacob to learn her secrets. Though she kept many, sharing a few with someone who seemed so distantly familiar came easily to her. And so, within a few minutes of talking they breached the subject of romance. She told him of her past love –her first– the one whose memory Jacob resurrected at the bhangra when he awkwardly announced himself. It was a story that she wanted to tell, though she often felt that few wanted to hear it.

They had met in college. She didn't know that she was beautiful until he told her so. She didn't need someone to do that for her now, of course, she told Jacob, but back then, as if it were a lifetime ago, she was still recovering from life in American Suburbia. Where everyone was white and no boys would date a gawky, brainy girl like her. "Brainy" was the epithet substituted for "brown". Or was it? She would never know she admitted.

Dresses grew sleeker, tops got tighter and shorts got shorter when she left home for college. And men, not boys, began to notice her. From "unattractive" she was upgraded to "picturesque" as white men would take her to beer bashes, finding that she served as a pleasing trophy of political progressiveness. Her status as picturesque came to an inglorious end when she found herself a little too frequently at the end of each social outing, hunched over and retching from too much confidence-building with warm, cheap beer.

Rumors spread. She withdrew socially for awhile, dressed in potato sacks and hid in her dorm room. It was during this time that she became more sure of herself, concentrating on her studies and allowing her intellect to develop along with her rounding hips and breasts. One sunny spring day, she decided to end her self-imposed reclusion. When she walked through campus in her brightly-colored, well-fitted sun-dress, she was beheld as a full-fledged sublime aesthetic experience by her fair-skinned classmates. A night with Sunita, even if only true in the boasting, was seen as a mark of sexual prowess. It was to come face to face with the terrible yet erotic, exotic power of the mysterious East. With Thaddeus, who was fundamentally a neo-Platonist when it came to dating, she found someone who seemed to intuitively grasp her essence. He grasped many more things as well, but he was able to see a profound beauty beneath her deliciously soft, brown skin.

They were a couple for the last two years of college and for a few months afterwards, when they moved in together. Sunita kept it a secret from her parents, but they found out eventually. How long could two people live together in absolute secrecy? They were bound to be discovered, despite their ambiguous answering machine messages, and Sunita's endlessly resourceful stalling of the nevertheless inevitable visit from her parents. When they did finally come, all of Thaddeus's possessions were stowed in the closet. ("I'm letting a friend store some things here. He's out of the country, and he really needs a hand," she told them). Eventually the great secret was revealed by a prying Indian woman, bitter about her denied membership bid into the Aunties, and seeking to draw their attention. (After uncovering Sunita's crime, she was quickly accepted into their ranks).

There were other pressures on their all-too-delicate affair. People stared at them when they walked hand in hand down the street. Older Indians, generously granting legitimacy, if not approval, assumed they were married. One kind gentle-

man who minded his son's Indian grocery would always ask
Sunita how her husband was doing whenever she came to the
store without Thaddeus. It all wore Sunita down. Thaddeus
didn't seem to notice the curious eyes—or perhaps he simply
didn't want to. When Sunita's parents did find out about her
romance, they brought up the uncomfortable question of
marriage.

The couple fought more. Perhaps it was because the
idyllic phase of their love had shattered under the pressure of
day to day living. But maybe –Sunita had to admit– it was
because of the strain caused by her desire to find out who she
was and where she came from. She ate more Indian food than
she ever had before: She extolled the medicinal properties of a
well-simmered dhal, claimed divine descent for the chili
pepper, and smiled exuberantly though unconvincingly as she
devoured a handful of sickly-sweet take-out jalebis. She read
the complete works of Gandhi, or tried to. She sat through
hour upon hour of Bollywood films, renting unwatchable
copies and forcing Thaddeus to watch them on their nights in.
She learned Hindi, Urdu, Telugu, Tamil and four other major
languages, or at least studied the fundamentals. Or learned a
couple of words in each. Actually, she only nearly mastered a
sentence or two in Hindi, though she could understand quite
a bit more. She would lay awake at night wondering where it
was that she truly belonged, as if such a place could really be.
Could it exist twelve thousand miles away, in another language, where everyone was the same color as she? "O India,
land of sages and seers, jungles, deserts and mountains! O
ancient land of my mother and sisters, father and brothers!"
She spoke with the poet's "o"—the o without the vulgar h,
besmircher of the ethereal. The one that begins such ugly
words: hell, hate, handout...Why had she changed so, trying
to become so much more Indian? Was she driven by guilt for
having lost something that was supposed to be in her care?
Was it because she never really belonged anywhere? Self-pity?
And perhaps the most painful question: Did she grow to love
all things Indian because her relationship with Thaddeus was

dying, or did their love sour because he could not understand her newfound nativism?

Thaddeus decided to move out. How could a Neo-Platonist boyfriend come to terms with the flux of identity and the search for an essence that could not be found? Why had the relationship failed? The old doubts resurfaced: Was it cultural? Was it racial?

He was working now in Colorado, or he was off trekking in Nepal, which he always talked about. Or he could have been struck by a speeding truck, flesh mangled and inseparable from metal parts. Funeral long over, now buried. Sunita didn't know what happened to him or where he was.

She stopped dreaming at night after he left her. It wasn't simply that she couldn't remember her dreams; her mind simply closed up shop as soon as her eyes shut and she began snoring. (She was a hearty snorer). No pleasant escapes to a wondrous dreamland where all wishes come true, no chances to fly through azure skies, to run in fields of dream-perfect smiling flowers. There were no wake-up-in-a-cold-sweat-but-oh-how-exciting nightmares. Not even a mundane replay of daily events on her internal T.V. set. She had stopped dreaming. After six months, The Dream came. It was the turning point. Too much emotional pressure had built up and forced a release, resulting in her worst nightmare ever. Or, perhaps, some impulse deep within her sounded a psychic alarm, warning the soul of its dangerous predicament: no Dreams, no Life.

Dream-Sunita was walking down a darkened hallway and then entered a room. A body, head bowed, broken neck in noose, hung from the ceiling. But what she saw was not a human body. It had a human shape, but its features were indistinguishable. A deep black interminable void, starless, lightless, had taken the shape of a body. After a moment of gaping, Sunita realized that there was something strangely familiar about it. Was it someone she knew? Dad? Mom? Thaddeus? No, none of them. But it seemed as if it were someone she knew. As she was drawn in and entered that void, she realized that the body was hers. She screamed. But the scream itself was swallowed by the darkness. She woke up, she thought, but she was still within in. She began to thrash and shout, but she could find no way out.

How she finally did awake from that dream that refused to end she couldn't remember. But she did awake. Shivering, sweating, and deeply terrified, she curled up in her bed and cried.

"That's when I decided to become angry. And that anger allowed me to survive, to fight the fall into nothingness. To fight for Myself," she told Jacob.

(She didn't tell Jacob about the conversation with her mother the next day, when she told her about The Dream.

"How about we buy you a car, Sunita?" said Dr. Chidhambaram.

"Mom! I don't want a car!"

"I know darling. Don't get mad at mummy. I only meant that it would be a distraction away from all of your depression. And all of these American boys. They're up to no good. Anyone who gives my little Sunita nightmares is no good, I tell you. No good! I'll ask your father as soon as he gets back from the hospital. He's been working so hard lately."

"You've been working hard too, Ma." Silence on the other end.

"Why don't you meet a nice boy?"

"Mom!" Protest.

"You're father thinks that its time you start thinking about marriage. You're father and I were talking, and we think you should go back to school, but then, honey, you should marry—"

"Mom!" Frustration.

"—A nice Indian boy."

"Mo-om!" Rising temper.

"Sunita, we're not getting any younger. And what about uma-ma? Don't you think your grandmother wants to see her first grandchild get married? I know what you're going to say, darling. But I have my duty as your mother! You can't stay alone forever and you've already been wasting your time with this boy."

"O.K. mom." Resignation. "I'll think about it. Love you. Bye."

Click. Lot of good that did, she thought. But Jacob knew nothing of all this).

After things ended with Thaddeus, she even more vigorously embraced her culture, seeking refuge in its grace and power. She frequented tanning salons to enhance her darkness in her "brown is beautiful" campaign. She pierced traditionally pierced body parts. She had her eyebrows threaded. She called her childhood Indian friends, seeking to compare experiences. She hoped for an explanation of who and what she was and why things went the way they did. She sought out that invisible minority beneath their baseball caps and college sweatshirts, beneath their neo-hippy, neo-conservative, neo-neon disguises in an attempt to find a common link, a refuge away from home, yet closer to it than wherever she had been.

Did Sunita and Jacob kiss and passionately embrace after her confession? Did they make love, their souls profoundly communicating in ways beyond mere words? Were the sparks of romance stoked to a brightly roaring bonfire? No they did not, and there was no active fire-tending. Jacob received not a peck on the cheek, though he had puckered his lips, while Sunita suffered the externally invisible ravages of a civil war between desire and resolution. She maintained her poise and told Jacob, "I'm sorry, I can't do this." Her reason? She no longer dated white men, she told him as delicately as she could. South Asian, East Asian, Southeast Asian, African, African-American, Latino, Middle Eastern, Native American, yes. White, no. Special exceptions were made for those of mixed descent, though the difficulties are obvious. She believed that it was the only thing she could do to protect herself.

"Anyway, Jacob," she said, composing herself, "since I've spilled my guts to you, you've got to tell me about yourself. Do you have any past loves or any secrets to tell?"

Tex ambled down the nearly empty Saturday-morning streets in his distinctive country-western gait, listening to the rhythmic click of his boot heels on the sidewalk. His very stride suggested the charm of country life to fastwalking city-dwellers. It was a sunny, peaceful morning. Car-horn-honkers had yet to take to the streets to claim right of way or to reprimand misbehaving drivers and pedestrians. And since it was Saturday, the annoying high-pitched beeping of multi-ton trucks driving in reverse down crowded alleys or streets was not to be heard. These were the kinds of mornings that Tex loved, and which so reminded him of home. But today, he was preoccupied and couldn't fully enjoy the morning. He was beginning to believe that his worst fears might come true—he would not win the bhangra bull-riding crown. And now, Sunita seemed to be paying far more attention to Jacob than was good for her. He wasn't jealous. He and Sunita had long ago settled the issue of romance between them. Well, it was more like she settled it. She firmly said, "No, Tex. How could I kiss a man who chews tobacco?" Tex knew that there were other reasons why their friendship had not blossomed into an affair, but he accepted her explanation almost grate-fully, and without probing the issue further. Since then, he had established himself as her confidant, and when he deemed it necessary, her protector.

He bought the city paper at the newsstand, leaned against a brick building and quickly thumbed through it. No news. He threw the paper into a nearby trash bin, and decided to walk the seven or so blocks to another vendor. The owner was Indian; he would stock at least a couple of the community papers.

Tex spit on a pigeon spreading its wings and puffing its chest out on the sidewalk in front of him. It fluttered and glared at him indignantly. There was a sharp note of menace in its cooing. Tex did not trust Jacob. He knew why Sunita felt the way she did, but it seemed like a foolish reason to get mixed up with someone who you just ran into at a bar, and who was left in an alleyway like a sack of garbage. Well, if she got into trouble, he'd be there for her. He felt his right biceps, and then his left, while he walked. His weight lifting phase had been over for at least a year, and he resigned himself to a life of scrawniness. But it didn't really matter....

Tex returned to the apartment a short while later. Sunita seemed preoccupied when she opened the door. "Hey, y'all," Tex said gregariously. "I've got some news. Nothing about the 'bhangra butcher' in the city paper. But there was something here in India Weekly." He held the paper aloft. Tex took a seat on the sofa chair, and began to rifle through the pages. "Let's see here...Look at this, a new Mr. India New Jersey was crowned in Newark. How about this, here in the Lone Star Beat..."

"Tex, is it about the bhangra?" Sunita asked.

"No, but I'll get to that. But ya'll gotta here this—

Several officials in a small town outside of Austin have been accused of involvement in an elaborate scheme of attempted assault. Austin is home to a growing Indian population lured by the promise of positions in the high-tech field. In a bloodthirsty ploy, city officials asked members of the Indian community to join a town celebration which included a reenactment of a historic battle between white settlers and Native Americans. The Indians were asked to play the role of the unfortunate Red Indians, which they were happy to do. The city officials, however, had allegedly substituted live ammunition for blanks. Luckily, no one was killed, though several suffered minor injuries. From the emergency room, electrical engineer Ravi Malwani said, "We were very happy to take part in their celebration, hoping to build bridges of communication and understanding. We were going to encourage their participation in our own India Day Parade. We had no idea it would turn out like this." The unfortunate father of two and active member of the community was still wearing ceremonial eagle-feather headdress when interviewed. After his arrest, one of the accused is quoted as saying, "It's high time we got rid of those heathen over-achievers."

"How about that!" Tex exclaimed enthusiastically, as he raised an empty soda can to his lips and expertly spit a thick brown liquid into it. He was chewing tobacco. He turned a few pages. "Here we go, bhangra coverage. I'm surprised to see it in here so quick. These guys are getting good. O.K. Let's see:"

Bhangra Butcher Still At-Large
Local police are still searching for clues in the brutal strangulation and robbery of the up and coming Sanskrit scholar Ephraim Stockwell, at the Global Beat Dance Club. Stockwell was attending a bhangra dance party for local Indian youths, organized by Rajeev Arora, of Edison, New Jersey. Police have released few details, and say that they have no suspects. However, one source in the police department has indicated that attention is being focused on the strange circumstances of the murder. Stockwell was garotted...

"What's garotted?"
"Strangled."
"Oh. Thanks."

Stockwell was garotted by a silk scarf with a coin fastened in it. Police officials speculate that the murder may be related to religious cult activities after interviewing Mr. Stockwell's mentor, noted Indologist, Professor Johannes Froese. Professor Froese has pointed out that the murderers emulated the methods of the Thugees, devotees of Goddess Kali. The Thugees were stamped out in British India through the efforts of the legendary Captain Sleeman under the administration of Governor-General Lord William Bentinck beginning in 1834.

"That is creepy," Tex remarked, after he finished reading the news story aloud. "Ya'll won't see this kind of thing down in Lubbock, I tell ya." He spit again.

"That *is* very strange," Sunita said, distractedly. Her curiosity had been aroused, and she began to process the details. "Jacob, I think you ought to tell Tex what you told me. About the Book, and the Library and all. It's better that we all know what 's going on." Tex politely listened while Jacob told his tale, that is, if one considers hawking and spitting tobacco-colored saliva polite.

Jacob had already told Sunita about the extraordinary turn that his life had taken in the last couple of months. He told her about Phoebe, and about the Librarian, though he left out some details of his last encounter with his mentor. He even told her about the Book, knowing that he risked ridicule. He was certain, though, to use phrases like "optical illusion" and "appearance of movement" to lend himself an air of objective distance. He was well aware of the danger he ran—it is not everyday that someone meets you at a night club and you reveal your experiences with the spirit world. It happened more than Jacob might think, but not without evoking some judgements on the teller's mental soundness. But he offered to show the Book to Sunita as proof.

For her part, Sunita reserved judgement. She was sympathetic to Jacob's story of what she sensed to be misguided love. And she knew that some things could be explained. Jacob had a very close relationship to his guru, and must have been going through a great deal of loss over his death. If he imagined some magical moment of transcendence, then that was fine. And if it really happened, if Jacob really had somehow reached to a higher spiritual plane, then that was O.K. too. She wasn't closed to the possibility of such a thing, just wary of fakes and over-enthusiastic New Agers. It was the Book that Sunita had a hard time believing, and despite Jacob's attempts to make himself sound less gullible than he did, she could tell how much he believed in its supernatural qualities. And Jacob seemed like a decent guy. She knew Tex wouldn't be so forgiving, but he had to be told. She wanted Tex to come along with Jacob and her when they went to the Library. She had taken a keen interest in Jacob's life, and wanted very much to figure things out.

After a private consultation with Tex in the kitchen, during which he offered to pay for lunch—she was on the job-search for "meaningful-work-before-more-school" after having quit yet another non-profit public interest organization in frustration—Sunita came into the living room and announced, "We're going for sushi. Do you wanna come?" Jacob politely refused, and said that he would like a chance to think a little about things while they were gone. Tex, still leery of Jacob, narrowed his eyes but said nothing. Sunita now trusted Jacob enough to leave him alone in her apartment for awhile. Whether she was motivated by an even stronger intuition of Jacob's trustworthiness, or she sensed that it would be silly to deny this request after disclosing her romantic history, Sunita herself was not certain. And she really didn't want Jacob to join them. A sushi lunch would be a good time to talk things over with Tex, though she already knew what he thought of Jacob's story.

Jacob was finally left alone. He lit the jasmine incense lying on Sunita's coffee table, and then sat on the floor. Legs crossed and hands brought together with fingertips touching, Jacob assumed a fairly uncomplicated asana. Eyes closed, he focused his attention on the single primordial syllable. OM. He eliminated all thoughts from his mind, shedding worries, desires, fantasies. OM he heard the sound as it resonated through his mind. The OM was not music; it was not to be listened to else he would imagine hearing fluctuations and tonal changes. It was a steady sound that must be heard. OM. The unmoving rhythm of the universe. OM. He became absorbed into the sound. The OM became Jacob and he became It. The OM became a single point of unseeable darkness. He was able to slip himself through the black point of light that was both the OM and himself. As he floated through the deep darkness, he began to form an image of the Librarian. He saw him; he felt his living presence.

When Jacob emerged from his deep meditation, he knew that he had communicated with his teacher. But he could only remember a few things, a few words that he knew he had so clearly heard spoken. "Take the path of action, Jacob," he told him. "The time for contemplation has passed. This is your rebirth. Do not mourn my death. Remember that time is circular, Jacob. I shall be reborn some day, we all shall be. But do not look for me in a single person. Do you think Creation would be so unoriginal?"

Jacob sat in silence, thinking over these words. When he opened his eyes, he found that Sunita and Tex had been patiently watching and waiting for him. As soon as she saw that Jacob had returned to normal consciousness, Sunita said to him, "You know, I've been thinking about something....Jacob, I think I might know your friend Phoebe."

6.

She lay with her head resting on his tight stomach muscles, her soft, shiny black hair draping his chest and arms. He held her hand, caressing it, and looked at the tattoo on her right shoulder blade, partially framed by splayed hair. Two almond shaped eyes, with thin, wavy eyebrows, and a nose like a tightly curled question mark. And in the center of what would be the forehead of the face, there was a small, shaded mark. He remembered once, he had begun to gently trace his finger over its lines while she was sleeping. She woke up suddenly, her eyes watering with uncontrollable rage, "Aloysius," she rebuked, "don't ever touch that again. Please, just don't do it. And don't ask me why..." One more secret that she kept from him. There were many other things that he was never to ask about. He stared at it now, but he knew if he did so too intently, she would feel it, and she would become angry.

Phoebe raised her head, and turned to him.. "Aloysius, what the hell went wrong?" she asked him. What had gone wrong? How did Jacob escape? Phoebe was worried. They weren't hiding; there was no one to suspect them of any wrongdoing. After the bhangra, they returned to Phoebe's apartment and made love, the excitement of dancing, music and murder and conspiracy still with them. How could Jacob have known of her plans? He must have known. He was proving to be a more formidable foe than Phoebe expected. Just how was he able to find and convince an understudy to be strangled in his stead? No one really knew about the murder except the Thugs, and she didn't tell Aloysius until yesterday night.

"I don't know, Phoebe, something went terribly wrong," he said, sadly. "You didn't tell me it was supposed to happen so soon—why didn't you tell me you put a contract out on him?"

"They got the wrong guy! Can you believe it? The wrong guy!—"

"Where did you find these thugs, anyway?"

"Old friends. There's something really familiar about that woman he was with—the one outside the club. I didn't really get a good look at her, but something about her seems so, I don't know, like I know her or something."

"I would have never figured he was out to screw you over, Phebe. You should be the one—I just can't believe it! What a motherfucker!"

"You know, Aloysius, we only did it that once."

"Yeah." Why did she still have to lie?

"You believe me, don't you?"

"Yeah, I believe you." He knew better, but what could he do? "Phebe, can't you just behave yourself?"

He always asked her to do that. But how could he expect monogamy from a high ranking member of a Tantric Sex Cult? He himself never fully embraced the left-handed sex practices despite his association with the Order. He was an exception to the membership rules. It was true that he practiced a little yoga, but more importantly, he was admired for cultivating the base emotion of anger. Anger was his tool, not lust. Aloysius did help Phoebe with her spiritual-physical work –he wanted to be supportive and sensitive– yet he always made the impossible request that she not pursue yogic power through sex. The contradiction of their relationship was obvious to him. Phoebe's intense sexuality was the source of his initial attraction to her, but it was a force over which he had no control. She caused him so much pain when she sought to increase her own power through carnal excess. One night stands he could put up with, but affairs lasting longer than a week drove him to a frenzy. Yet Phoebe also calmed his anger, cooling his soul, and preventing him from burning himself up.

Phoebe went for a shower. Aloysius knew she wasn't telling him everything, but it was better not to push too hard. "Doctrine!" she lectured the night before on the way to the Library. "It's all about a new doctrine for the Order. That old man has been running things his way for a long time—all this couples in a cubicle crap! How many graduate on to Nirvana? Hardly any in years. Just think of the shakti released in an all-out orgy! He's so old-fashioned he can't take it. Look how he handled this whole Jacob thing. He didn't even tell us about him. The old man wasn't even going to let us meet him until I raised hell about it. To think, I trusted him once—"

"So you want to kill Jacob?"

"We have to. Before the Librarian leaves his body. You know what it means if he uses Jacob—it will change him. It has to. You can't be around that old man when he reaches that kind of transcendence without it changing you. He will definitely be harder to handle."

"I don't know Phoebe..."

"What do you mean, you don't know? You never understand these religious matters. Jacob is going to seize control one of these days, and it might be sooner than you think. If he does, we'll never have a say in anything anymore. God! I just hate myself for making love to him, having him inside of me, touching me—"

"I'm going to kill that goddamn motherfucker..."

Phoebe rolled her head back, wetting her hair. Oh how much she would rather have had a bath! To lay back and close her eyes, to ease her tense muscles and clean her pores, after treating her hair with Parachute Coconut Oil, the secret to her hair's bright Oriental sheen. She was in a bit of a hurry today, so a shower would have to do. Things were happening much sooner than she expected, and plans had to be made immediately. She kneaded her shoulder and neck muscles under the showerhead. She had to be relaxed before the orgy; overanxiousness might make her appear weak, and she could not afford to look so in front of her future disciples. The Librarian, that cunning, crafty man, had passed on so soon, without even the slightest clue that it would be last night. But the old man must have known that Phoebe was going to make a move soon. She lathered the papaya conditioning shampoo into her hair, which would leave it smelling like a basket of exotic fruit. How did Jacob know? He had spent so much time with the Librarian, no doubt learning all manner of secret arts and incantations, being groomed for power. But Jacob kept his lessons a secret from her. Yet she knew, even when she set up the accidental discovery by Aloysius, that he was nearly ready for succession to cult leadership. What a double-crossing manipulative sonofabitch! She was tensing up again, fiercely squeezing the shampoo through her hair and vigorously rubbing her fingers on her scalp. But the rich, fruity scent began to calm her, the smell of papaya, mango and the slight hint of apricot. She began to more delicately work the shampoo through her hair, relaxing, remembering....

For all the time she had known him, the Librarian was never able to exert much control over her, even before Aloysius. She and the old man had been much closer back then. She remembered how they met: Browsing in the natural aphrodisiac section of a health food store, she reached for the vial of damiana leaf, and he for the bottle of the marapauma-cataaba blend. Their eyes met...She was going to be the one, he promised her. He trained her, they practiced the left-handed rituals—all of them. When Aloysius had come into her life, the old man suddenly became cold to her. She was no longer his favorite. While her relationship with him was deteriorating, Phoebe introduced Aloysius to the other members of the Order. One thing the Librarian couldn't do was to deny Aloysius's spiritual strength. But he couldn't tolerate sharing his favorite pupil, so he chose the only weapon that he could use against her: he denied her the right of succession. Banishing her from the Order was out of the question since Phoebe and also Aloysius had already quickly become powerful, respected members, despite some grumbling to the contrary. (Phoebe was adept at 726 asanas, could levitate, and was said to have flown from peak to peak, without the assistance of aircraft, in Nepal several years ago. Although Phoebe's exhibition was reported as fact in the cult newsletter, wagging tongues did suggest that the Nepali villagers were unreliable. "Bribery," they whispered. It wasn't only Phoebe's heretical tendencies that caused cult members to assume the raised-eyebrows-in-dissapproval asana; she earned not a few enemies because of her ambitiousness). His reprisal? Unable to make her do as he wished, the Librarian had to outfox her—which is exactly what he did with Jacob. She rinsed her hair, and washed the soap from her body. She was not going to let the old man get away with it. The answer was simple—seize control of the Order and rid herself of Jacob. Determined, she turned off the water, and pulled open the shower curtain.

She reached for her towel and dried herself. After stepping out of the tub, she stood in front of the mirror, which had fogged up from the shower's hot steam. Looking into her medicine cabinet, she reached for the plastic bottle of baby oil, and then let her towel drop to the floor. Her skin had to be as soft and smooth as could be for the orgy today. She poured some of the oil into the palm of her hand, and bending over, she rubbed it up and down her long legs, concentrating on knees and ankles. Coarse, dry skin might cause a bad kind of friction, and the slightest displeasure could kill concentration during the orgy. She took more oil into her hands and massaged it into her arms, and her stomach, and on her breasts. She smoothed oil on her hips, and then her thighs, and then followed the muscle lines up to her stomach. She dabbed some onto her index finger, and tickled each of her aureoles and nipples. Her skin moist and silky, almost glistening, she reached for her hair brush and combed through her soft, clean hair. Talcum powder came next, which she sprinkled all over her body, leaving the floor dusty with the excess.

Phoebe put her bathrobe on, and went into the bedroom, where she found Aloysius working up a sweat doing pushups. "What are you pissed off about now?" she asked him.

"Nothing. Fifty-three. Fify-four. Just working off some tension. Fifty-six."

"Can you please stop at sixty. I have to talk to you."

"Right. Sixty. Done."

"Aloysius, we need to get rid of him."

"Right. What do you want me to do?"

"I'm going to call the Thugs. You just sit tight. No more mistakes. I've got an orgy at noon. I've got to get going."

"Great." Aloysius dropped back down to the floor and began doing pushups again.

"Cut that out. You're impossible. Anyway, that little upstart is finished. We can't afford to have him around." She walked over to the night table and picked up the telephone. She needed to get things straightened out before the first love-in.

In a live-work space across town, sixteen turbaned men sat on a blanket, gathered around a pickaxe, a silver medallion, a pile of coarse sugar and a flower-pot full of soil. "Blessed is the Goddess!" called out their leader, facing west, head tilted to the skies. His prodigious hooked nose formed a forty-five degree angle with the ground. He scratched out a tiny hole in the soil with his long, bony index finger, and dropped in a few grains of the sugar. "Blessed is the Goddess! May you provide as many riches as you did for the great Jora Naick and Koduk Bunwaree." The others repeated his words, calling out the names of the illustrious forefathers they claimed for their own. Hooked Nose sprinkled water on the pickaxe and the flower pot, and then dropped in a few grains of sugar in each of the followers hands. "*Tobako kha lo!*" ("Eat your tobacco!") someone shouted, giving the usual signal for the commencement of ritual murder. But it wasn't time to kill; it was time to eat the consecrated sugar, their offering to the Goddess, and their reward for the killing. Its exquisite sweetness gave them strength and courage, and proved the rightness of their cause.

It also brought them visions. Some saw themselves surrounded by mounds of gold and silver coins, and suitcases full of hundred dollar bills. They sat upon golden thrones, and extravagant feasts were set out before them...Others saw the Thugs of Ancient India, from whom they borrowed their practices (everybody needs heroes), offering their hands in friendship to travelers, only to deceive them, repaying their trust with murder and theft. They too sat together and tasted the great *goor*, the sweetest of all sugars, which drove pity and remorse from the hearts of those who tasted it....

To the most fortunate, the Mother Goddess, dreadful, terrible, powerful Kali appeared. She battled the Great Demon, slashing at her foe with a weighty sword. But from each drop of the Demon's blood that fell to the ground, yet another demon would arise. Kali, in her infinite wisdom and resourcefulness, created two men and gave them each a silk cloth to strangle the demon's progeny. Killing without bloodshed, these first Thugees earned the gratitude of Kali, who rewarded them by sanctioning their trade of theft and murder. The mighty, victorious Kali appeared again in their vision, waving her sword through the air, her belt of human skulls shaking from her fury...

The telephone rang. Hooked nose rose and went into his office. He took his turban off, exposing his long, prematurely gray hair bundled on the top of his head. Turbans were now only used for rituals. He picked up the phone.

"Hello. It's me."

"Hello, Ms. Kelli. *Aulae Bahin, Ram, Ram*," he said, speaking the traditional Thug greeting in their secret dialect of *Ramasee*.

"*Aulae Bhae, Ram, Ram*," she responded.

"We were just performing the *tuponee*. Ah, it's a lovely ritual, you know, Miss Kelli, performed after a successful sacrifice, since, well, since the very beginning. A nice ceremony always brings a smile to my face. You know, I was just thinking—"

"You've heard what's happened?"

"Yes, yes. I was told just a short while ago. Ms. Kelli, you know how bad things have been. We don't like these contract jobs, but it's very difficult to do anything else these days. Do you know how hard it is for six turban-wearing hitchhikers to be picked up, no matter if we tell them it's for their own safety? So many of the old ways, gone...This is a no good country."

"Oh, Ameer, where did you get that accent?" Phoebe teased.

"Practice, Miss, practice. It makes everything a little more authentic."

"Anyway, you stopped wearing turbans in public years ago—"

"True, Miss, true. But many other things have changed also...I swear on the sacred pickaxe, Miss, we never even have time for the proper burial."

"What went wrong, last night, Ameer?" she asked, serious once again.

"We went to the nightclub just as you told us, and we went to the agreed place. The fellow was a little rounder than you described, but we thought it must be him. Who else could it be? We spoke to him very little, and then it was time...."

"Are you sure you can trust all of your people, Ameer? I think someone might have tipped Jacob off about our plans—"

"Oh, no, Miss. No one dares such treachery and tastes the *goor*—I will see them and feel them. There is no way to escape. Besides, no one leaves without my knowledge, and I have the only phone, which is kept in my locked office. Ah, Miss," Ameer sighed. "I should have known that something would go wrong. There was an omen, you see, a very bad omen."

"What omen?"

Ameer mumbled inaudibly.

"Speak up, Ameer, what was the omen?"

"I said, a hare scampered across the road in front of us on the way to the club. From left to right, Miss. Left to right! It is a very bad omen. It could mean our ruin—"

"Look, I've got to go. I'll be in touch." She was losing her patience.

"You don't understand, Miss. The hare! The omen of the—"

Click.

It was almost noon, and Phoebe was directing the mopping up operations at the Library. Those in deep meditation were awakened from their trances, yogis were unknotted and told to stand upright, and couples who had been copulating for months were separated. Phoebe was making preparations for the orgy. A few protested, and Phoebe had them thrown out of the Occult Sciences section, and from the Order. One feisty, toothless octogenarian chose to make a stand and refused to leave his cubicle. He screamed out, "Heresy! Heresy!" when he heard rumor of Phoebe's plans. He was no match for Phoebe's growing band of henchman, and so his rebellion proved fruitless. They wrestled him to the ground with little difficulty, and two of the toughs sat on his chest until he gasped a promise to leave quietly. His nineteen year old partner, an exchange student from a yoga college in Marin County, California was thrown out along with him, lest she begin spreading his seditious lies.

Soon the cubicles were cleared, and the followers assembled on the gymnasium mats provided for the event. Most were naked or nearly so, all of them wiry thin, superhumanly flexible, and many wore their hair in dreadlocks. It was a sight that Phoebe dreamed of for a long time: amongst this crowd of more or less eager followers stood the most advanced members of the cult. Phoebe took her position in front of them, standing on a small raised platform constructed for this day. "I am the new leader!" she declared to approving cheers.

But when she announced that the Order would be shifting its focus from couples to mass orgies, an anxious silence fell over the crowd. Many of them were reluctant to embark on the new path set by Phoebe, both from force of habit and the fear that it may very well be heretical. Others blushed and giggled nervously, which Phoebe took as a positive sign. It was quite a feat to embarrass these tantric practitioners; they were hardly known for their modesty.

Phoebe was to win the day.   It was true that she was feared by many of the rank and file members of the Order. Her intelligence, her beauty, and of course her yogic powers could easily intimidate these people who so craved forceful leadership, and without the stronger, more established figure of the Librarian, she was impossible to resist. And she knew how to exploit their love for him for her own ends. She told them that the orgies were indeed his wish and that he had planned to introduce them to the practices of the Order very soon, but passed on before he could. Since they were technically both in mourning for his death and celebrating his advancement to a higher plane of existence, no one dared refuse his last wishes.

"Let us begin the divinely sanctioned orgy!" Phoebe shouted excitedly. She called out instructions, and soon everyone was in place. It was noon exactly.

Now Brother Govind knew of Phoebe's lie, but he said nothing. He kept guard at the entrance to the Hall of Cubicles, and, well, he was permitted to watch the orgy. He had no real reason to complain—and he saw what happened when you complain. Tossed out onto the street naked.

Meanwhile, Aloysius sat at his regular table, with a cup of espresso at the Cafe Feu d'Amour. He checked his watch. Noon. He breathed deeply, and then pursed his lips.

Back in the Library, legs and arms jumbled indiscriminately, and genitalia belonging to both genders found ways to enter or be entered. The mass of bodies began to undulate. They grunted and groaned, and simultaneously chanted the sacred mantra. Industrial size fans, set on the perimeter of the mats blew air over the overheating bodies. As the group uttered a collective sigh of pleasure, an aura of golden light emerged around the tangled bodies.

Now fully dressed, and energized by the forces released by the orgy, Phoebe sat at the desk once occupied by the Librarian. She picked up his phone and dialed a number quite familiar to her. "I've got some work for you to do," she said into the receiver.

"No problem, Miss, no problem," the man replied, running his fingers through his long, ashen-grey hair.

7.

*T*ex, Sunita, and Jacob sat in the cab of the cherry red pick-up truck. Decorative license plates, "his" on the driver's side, and "hers" on the passenger were set in the rear window. Tex's brother Sunil loaned the truck to him. Business was good; he already had enough cars parked in the circle driveway of his ranch-style home. The plates were his, and Tex was forbidden to remove them. There was actually no "her" to claim the passenger side. Sunil was still unmarried, though the chances of arranging a bride from India already decked out in boots and spurs was increasing with each passing day. Waiting for that day when his parent's queries would be answered, or he received positive response to his internet matrimonial, Sunil let the spot be occupied by his golden brown German Shepherd, Wadha, whom he named after his favorite South Indian dish, that deep fried dumpling which, when properly prepared, reached the same hue as its canine namesake. Tex was allowed to make some changes to the borrowed vehicle—the gun rack was taken down, and a sticker, edited with Tex's Bowie knife, was placed on the rear bumper: "Don't Mess With Tex—" it warned.

The threesome were on their way to the Library to take a look at the Book Jacob had mentioned. Jacob needed to establish some credibility with his new friends. If he couldn't get past Govind to show them the cult's cubicles, he might at least be able to find the Book, and prove its powers. "Did the police get the Librarian's body out?" he wondered. Who do you call when someone dies? Jacob always only passively experienced death—distant relatives and friends of the family passed on, but he was never called upon to dispose of the body and alert the authorities. Did Phoebe and Aloysius take care of it? "Wait! Jacob shouted. "I have to feed my cat! We have to go to my place." Tex listened to directions, and Sunita remained silent on the way to Jacob's apartment, except for one disdainful remark aimed at Jacob. "You're a cat person?" she said with nose wrinkled.

It had been quite awhile since Jacob had guests. Even Phoebe insisted that they always meet at her apartment. Jacob fully expected to be attacked by Nicodemus, and indeed, had awkwardly offered a few words of explanation to Sunita and Tex, hoping to forestall the inevitable embarrassment of Nicodemus's customary greeting. Cautiously opening the door, Jacob was pleasantly surprised to see a subdued Nicodemus lying upon the couch, nonchalantly yawning in acknowledgment of Jacob, his provider and protector. No cat eyelashes were batted in jealousy at either Sunita or Tex.

Excusing himself to change from Aloysius's clothes into his own, Jacob found a suitable pair of jeans and a t-shirt in the dresser drawer next to his bed, and then went into the bathroom, leaving Sunita and Tex behind to inspect his Spartan quarters. Tex, holding a tobacco chewers disdain for smokers, considered the ashtrays full of cigarette butts one more point in Jacob's disfavor. Sunita found the sheer number of Jacob's books fascinating: Books on shelves, books on the floor, books on the kitchen counter, and books on his bed. Always impressed with a fellow reader, she mouthed a "wow" to Tex, who pointed to the cigarette butts expecting her to share his disapproval. She ignored him and walked up to one of the shelves and began reading the spines.

Jacob emerged from the bathroom, picked up his tobacco pouch from the floor and rolled a cigarette. "I hope you don't mind," and went by the open window to smoke. "I think you two are going to really find this fascinating. It has changed my life. I felt completely reborn after I was given that book, and met the Librarian."

Nicodemus fed and watered, the threesome got into the pickup truck and headed for the Library. It was time for Sunita to tell the others how it was that she knew Phoebe. She was certain that the woman who rode past in the Lexus the night before was the same woman she had known two years before. She couldn't really see her at first, but now, after replaying the scene in her mind, she was sure. But Phoebe didn't go by that name when Sunita knew her. She used to be called Jasmine. Jasmine Sunflower. She had come to a local university to lecture on yoga. It was the kind of talk that attracted both New Agers and a few curious Indians here and there, Sunita explained, feeling the need to justify her presence there. At the time it seemed like a legitimate step in the her quest to realize her ethnic identity.

Jasmine stood out far above the usual dilettantes who tried to pass themselves off as yoga adepts not only because of her great flexibility but also because she was such a compelling speaker. Her unconventionality quickly became apparent when she argued that violence could be a means of yoga. But she did not stop with the mere advocacy of violence for personal salvation—she insisted that force was necessary to spread the word of yogas salvific power. To further the cause of the Universal Life Force, it would be acceptable to coerce the reluctant to practice yoga, and if need be, to wrap their legs around their necks, bludgeoning them until they repeated the sacred mantras. One wouldn't expect the crowd at a lecture on yoga and meditation to be too receptive to the message of inner peace through violence, but after a few shocked gasps, and a couple of huffy walkouts by the self-proclaimed orthodox, Jasmine was given the chance to fully explain her theories to an extremely receptive audience.

Jasmine was a captivating woman. Articulate. Beautiful. And she had the ability to almost control the thoughts of the audience when she spoke. Was it mass hypnotism? The beguiling magic of a yogini? Or like so many coarse dema-gogues, did she simply say what the people wanted to hear, appealing to their baser instincts? Sunita didn't know. But she saw that people loved her. Sunita stayed and listened to her talk—of course she had retained her critical distance and objectivity, she assured Jacob and Tex—but she wanted to hear what Jasmine had to say. Some of it did truly make sense, and well, the violence was something with which she didn't fully agree, but it was all on a theoretical level, and seemed largely for rhetorical effect. Perhaps, Sunita finally allowed, she was hoping that her rage over Thaddeus might find a way to focus itself. Anyway, after the lecture, Sunita waited for the crowd to clear, and then introduced herself to Jasmine.

"But what I can't believe, Jacob," Sunita said, interrupting her story, "is that you fell for that 'ashram to ashram' crap."

"What do you mean?" Jacob nervously asked.

"I mean what I said, Jacob. It's a load of crap. A lie. I remember she used to tell that story to people all the time to get their sympathy. It was one of the reasons we ended our friendship."

Yes, Sunita and Jasmine were friends for a short while, maybe a couple of months at most. "I learned a lot from her, or at least, thought I was learning something," Sunita explained. "A lot about self-control, independence. Those are good things, and I needed more of them. But she was so angry about something, something that happened to her. But she never told me what it was, or really even admitted it. But I could sense it."

It was true, Jasmine's parents were wandering hippies. They did love her, though perhaps their minds were fuzzy from too much acid in their younger days to be the ideal parents. They did somewhat curtail their itinerant ways when their precious Jasmine was born, though it would be years before they finally settled down, well into Jasmine's teenage years. Not only did they love their daughter, they were indeed the ones who first introduced her to so many of the customs and so much of the knowledge of the East: her mother had given birth to Jasmine while a Ravi Shankar eight-track tape played in the background, synchronizing her contractions with the tabla's increasing tempo. (It was a home delivery). Sunita knew that Jasmine's parents were kind, loving people, and that they cared very deeply for their daughter. And they were quite proud of her for choosing a career as a nurse. "A nurse?" Jacob asked incredulously. She had to tell them something, and since she knew so much about physiology, it seemed a natural cover. Saying she was a doctor would have stretched the truth a little too much, and she did still need to borrow money from time to time. Jasmine at some point in her life –Sunita did not know exactly when or how it happened– came to resent her parents a great deal. But was Sunita right? Was there a single traumatic moment that had changed Phoebe's entire life, rendering her, in Sunita's words, "untrustworthy, bitterly angry and relentlessly manipulative"? Perhaps it was because her parents had moved around so much, never able to offer a stable environment in which the young Jasmine could grow. Or, indeed, as Sunita offered years ago, reading glasses set on her nose, and assuming her relationshp-analytical mode, "Phoebe's dysfunctionality may have been born from a broader socio-cultural malaise that threatens the utter breakdown of Western values." Whatever "it" was, Jasmine had emerged from a not-quite model childhood into a lonely, troubled adulthood. But, she was not the only one. Now, the question that Sunita sometimes wondered since she ended her relationship with Phoebe: would freshly hyphenated immigrants be spared from such a moral anomie?

"Anyway, we had a falling out, and completely lost touch with each other. I hadn't seen her since then, until the other night. But this violence stuff scares me a little. I kind of think that she might be wrapped in all of this....There was something really strange about her voice when she saw us outside of the club."

"I think she might be in trouble," Jacob said, offering his explanation.

"If you say so, Jacob." She paused, weighing her next words. "There's a dark side to her. I don't know if you are willing to see it."

"A dark side to *her*!" Tex thought, but said nothing. "What about Jacob!" But Tex kept his mouth shut. Sunita already knew what he thought of Jacob. What troubled him more now was that he had never heard Sunita's story before, though he had prided himself on knowing everything, on being her most intimate confidant.

With the luck of a rural newcomer to the city, Tex found a parking space across from the Library, a massive, gray concrete building. A veritable fortress of learning. Passing through the entrance turnstiles, they entered the lobby and main reading room. Rows of wooden file cabinets containing the card catalogs stood to the left. Next to them were a dozen or so computer stations able to access billions of electronic impulses conveying tiny bits of information of every aspect of human knowledge and every moment of recorded human history, or learned speculations regarding what was not preserved. Long wooden reading tables were arranged in rows to the right. The room was unexpectedly airy, the fifty feet high ceiling allowing it to circulate. What struck Sunita immediately was how ordinary everything had seemed so far—there were no sightings of robe-clad cult members or fraudulent sannyasis in the lobby. Not a clue to the phenomena, now "alleged" in Sunita's mind-speech, that Jacob claimed to be a part of was to be gleaned from the perfectly normal exterior, or library entranceway, or even the lobby. Library personnel busily checked out stacks of books to patrons, an odd bookworm here and there carried two dozen or so volumes in shopping bags. There was no sinister activity whatsoever.

Jacob led them to the entranceway to the bookstacks. Once inside the book stack area, the true size and complexity of the building became apparent. Millions upon Millions of volumes were housed here, from dusty, moldy books filled with decaying pages that were hardly ever taken down from their shelves to more or less recent bestsellers. After walking down a couple of aisles, and taking a left, and then a right, they reached an elevator that was, despite its obscurity, the only one up to the floor that held the Occult Sciences section. Once they reached the correct level, they walked down a few more aisles, took a couple more left and right turns, and then went up a flight of stairs, and followed more corridors until finally reaching the chain linked fence door that led to the Occult Sciences Area, and the old man's desk that sat in front of it. Jacob could never remember the original path he had taken on the first day he met the Librarian, who showed him the special elevator afterwards.

Jacob searched the Librarian's desk, but it had been cleared, except for the telephone. No official library personnel were present to open the door or to bear witness, so Tex volunteered to pick the fence door lock with his multi-purpose pocket knife. "Something I learned to do when a bunch of us went down to Laredo to raise some hell. Ya'll just re-lax now," he told them. Why such a skill was learned in Laredo, and to what schoolboy's misdemeanor it was put in the service of he didn't say. But the task was completed soon enough, and the three began to peruse the shelf for what Jacob still insisted to be the aptly titled *Book of Truth.*

Tex and Sunita searched together, both half-heartedly. If they stuck together, they secretly reasoned, they might manage a full heart of enthusiasm. They weren't much help to Jacob, and indeed they rolled their eyes in unison with every third title that they read. Meanwhile, Jacob searched earnestly, systematically reading the titles of each of the books on the shelf. He wondered how it was that he had let it slip from his mind so, for that was exactly what had happened. He had brought it back to the Librarian when they began meeting, and he never thought to ask about it again. Its magic had been much less compelling than his guru, the living source of knowledge. So much else had happened in the last couple of months, too. In the back of his mind he always thought that if needed to he would be able to find it. And he remained confident that the Librarian was day by day unraveling its magic while teaching its exoteric lessons.

After several minutes, Jacob called out excitedly, "It's here!" Tex and Sunita found find Jacob seated on the floor, with the book open in his hands. They crouched down beside him, positioning themselves to see it perform its magic. First Jacob showed them the handwritten note that had been placed in front of the book as if to prove its authenticity. And then he flipped through several pages, excitedly repeating the phrase, "Yes, yes, this is it." He finally opened the book to its center, and held it flat in his hands, waiting, staring. But nothing happened. Of course, he explained, how could they expect something so quickly. Tex stood up, and walked a few paces and then sat down again, gently leaning against one of the stacks. Sunita relaxed, and dropped down from her haunches until she sat flat on the floor, hoping to ease Jacob's performance anxiety, but knowing that nothing would happen. Things like this just didn't happen, she thought to herself, no matter how much you want to believe. They waited. And waited. Jacob waited because he had to prove something to his new friends, and now, himself. Sunita waited out of sympathy for Jacob, wanting something to happen for his sake. And Tex waited because Sunita waited; there would be time for vocalizing the stupidity of waiting later in private. But for now, for whatever individual reason, they waited. And waited. Nothing happened. Jacob all the while stared intently at the page, blinking rarely, reluctantly.

"I don't understand it. Nothing is happening!" Jacob finally said.

"The original must have been replaced by an exact, nonfunctioning facsimile. "The fiends!" said Tex. Without a hint of mercy. Jacob's first thought: "That's a possibility." Second: "Sarcastic son of a bitch."

"Look, Jacob, there was probably a spell put on it. You know, a hex, a spell..." Sunita offered, as delicately as she could. What she didn't say but thought: "And they probably put a hex on you too, Jacob. How could believe this stuff?" Sunita believed most of Jacob's story, and she didn't want to see him so distraught. It was better to find some sort of rational explanation.

"Why do you have to show us the Book Jacob?" Sunita finally asked. "I mean, do we really have to see it do the things you said it did?"

"If I show it to you, I can prove that it's true."

"Jacob, we believe you –we do– a lot of what you say. Why don't you show the cubicles, show us the cult—Let's see something we can believe."

"You know, I didn't think it was true myself at first."

"Then you can understand why we say this.... Jacob, it's just that there is so much that is out of the ordinary.... Maybe you wanted to believe this most of all—"

Book set aside, Jacob led the doubters to the cubicles, promising a shocking display of wanton sex and chanting yogis. Expecting vindication, Jacob was greatly disappointed to find the cubicles completely empty of cult members. Not a single salacious sadhu was to be seen. Now it was true that the presence of such cubicles might be an architectural oddity, but it certainly did little to verify Jacob's story. Jacob was on the verge of panic, and Sunita began to question her faith in him. She was expecting to be led to the beating heart of a fully operating sex cult. It was then that Tex called attention to the floor mats and the industrial fans, which were turned off, else they would have been noticed immediately. All eyes had been on the cubicles when they first walked in, and few other details were processed. Yet, floor mats and industrial fans do not a sex cult make. Out of place in a library, but not convincing evidence to those skeptical of the occult and the supernatural, or at least unfamiliar with non-Occidental, diasporic religious orders.

Tex wandered about the hall a bit more, and then came across an unnatural sight that would haunt him for weeks to come. Off to side of one of the fans lay a tremendous pile of latex condoms—used—and not disposed of properly. "Hey, y'all, look at this..." he hollered. Sunita blurted out, "That is absolutely disgusting!" and Jacob simply nodded, but could not conceal his self-satisfied smile. "Well, something certainly went on here," Tex announced. And then said thoughtfully, "At least these crazies practice safe-sex."

Then entered a rubber-gloved Govind, pushing a janitor's cart, equipped with mop, broom, bucket, state-of-the-art cleaning products, and plastic garbage bags.

"Nobody's not allowed here!"

"Ah-ha! So what you're saying, partner, is that we *are* allowed in here." Govind looked hurt. He had always been a nervous fellow, easily bruised. Jacob shook his head to Tex, trying to prevent what he feared might come next—either a debate on the finer points of Govind's self-designed Via Negativa, or a hurt, angry, hostile Govind, insulted by Tex's challenge. But Tex took Jacob's gesture as a sign of encouragement.

"You see, partner, a double-negative forms a positive. So we are allowed in here."

"Yes. Exactly—a positive. Nirvana!" Govind smiled beatifically. "But nobody's not allowed. Sri Phoebe's orders."

Sunita had been ignoring Tex's display of dialectical skill and instead spent her time giving Govind a good looking-over. Here was a cult-crazy if she ever saw one. Govind had untufted his hair at Phoebe's behest, but remained nude. And now he smeared his entire body with grey ash, also by Phoebe's order. She had no particular purpose in asking him to do so, but it was part of her policy of overturning the old order. Govind gladly obliged.

"Where is everybody, Brother Govind?" Jacob asked.

"Gone. Nowhere. Not here any more."

"Where did they go? And Govind, what happened here?"

"Sri Phoebe's changing everything. Sent everybody out— recruiting drive." Whispering in nervous excitement, he continued, "Big orgy here. Shakti tornado! Nobody's supposed to know nothing....Are these friends of yours?" Govind asked suspiciously.

"Yes, Brother Govind."

"Nice. Very nice," he said, looking at Sunita. He stuck his tongue out. She winced. Jacob turned to her and explained, "It means he likes you—"

"I know *that*, Jacob. But it's not at all flattering!"

"No, Sunita, you don't understand. It's Tibetan."

"Uh-huh."

"Now, Jacob, you have to get out of here. Sri Phoebe doesn't like you anymore..."

Govind turned around and began to sweep the mats. Tex, Sunita and Jacob held conference.

"Let's get out of here, Jacob. I get a bad feeling from this place," Sunita said.

"I'm with her."

"Did you hear what he said? She doesn't like me anymore! And what's this orgy business! That's forbidden..."

"Look, how about we get out of here, and stop somewhere for take-out samosas and mango lassis? I'm fixing to keel over from hunger. Whaddya say, Sunita?"

They left a naked Govind, kneeling on hands and knee, scrubbing the floor mats with a sponge.

8.

$h$ooked Nose, sat in his tiny office, leaning back in his chair, holding open an Indian emigre newspaper. His office was attached to the larger space where rituals and meetings were held, and where the other Society members slept and ate. His desk was cluttered with papers. Order forms for equipment (mostly scarves and knives), Society memoranda, expense account receipts, etc. A calendar, with dates of expeditions marked, hung on the wall. Auspicious days were starred, inauspicious ones were colored in with black ink. The small library in the office was comprised mostly of writings on the historical Thugs, composed by the forces of law and order. His most prized volume was the *Handbook for the Modern Thug,* which he had himself assembled after painstaking research.

Today, there was much to be concerned about. That little mistake at the bhangra a week ago had caused much more trouble than he had expected. He knew it was a risky job, but he had accepted it anyway. Phoebe, with all her faults, could be so compelling sometimes. It was impossible to say no. Besides, she offered such a generous donation. He ran his fingers through his long hair, now dyed with henna. Disguise seemed a necessity. He was confident that the authorities didn't know who or where his Society was. But it was clear that they knew that a group of Thugs was responsible. That was enough to make him nervous. No one had ever suspected a thing before. Until now, he and his clan had made their sacrificial killings without leaving any clues and raised no suspicions. The murders were blamed on friends, relatives, so-called business associates, or were said simply to be random acts of urban violence. This time, though, he had gotten so spooked at such a public job that he left behind a scarf. And now they knew that somewhere in this city a group of Thugs roved the city streets, stalking the weak and helpless.

"Just look at this nonsense!" he called out to the tall, muscular blond-haired, blue-eyed man of Nordic descent guarding his door. "Come in here and listen to this!"

Noted Indologist Speaks Out
on Thuggee Murder

Well respected Indologist Johannes Froese delivered a public lecture at Broadview University earlier this week entitled "Thuggee Murders in America: Definitive Evidence of the Resurgence of the Cult of Thieves and Stranglers." Professor Froese pointed to the recent murder of Ephraim Stockwell, an up and coming scholar of Sanskrit who was brutally murdered at a bhangra dance party at the Global Beat Dance club. (Details of the murder were reported in last week's issue). A secret society, the professor says, has organized in the United States and is copying the methods of India's Thuggee murders....

"Blah, blah, blah. Look at this... 'Professor Froese is taking his findings to the people because the police have ignored clear evidence of cult activity.' A damned, self-righteous fanatic. He should mind his own business."

"Absolutely right, sir, absolutely right. Mind his own business."

"Well, look at this. Maybe somebody will put him in his place...."

Committee Formed to Combat Bad Publicity

Pointing to the negative images created in media and in recent hostile reports by "noted academics who are nothing but sensationalists," a group of prominent Indo-Americans have formed a committee to promote a positive public image of Indians living in America. "Most Indians are hard-working, responsible citizens, said keynote speaker Dr. Nilesh Patel at the inaugural meeting of the Committee for the Positive Public Image of Indians

Living in America (CPPIILA). "*It is very difficult for we as a community to gain the political power we need for our voices to be heard when we always face negative public images in the media. Indians are poor. Indians are superstitious. Indians are backwards. We always hear this on the six o'clock news. But it is time to stop making Indians look bad.*" *It is expected that the CPPILA will target the upcoming lecture tour "Killers for Kali" planned by the famous Indologist Johannes Froese....*

"Can't ask for anything better than that, don't you think. Put that nosey nut-case in his place!"

"It is time," interrupted another blonde assistant, speaking through the slightly opened   door.

Fifteen Thugs sat in a circle in the center of the room. Hooked Nose, a.k.a. Ameer, took a quick head count. "Where is Ramesh?" he asked. At that moment, the Thug in question took his place in the circle, appearing dazed and glassy-eyed. Ramesh had been watching the Pan-Asian Channel for any news coverage of the Stockwell fiasco. Not a single relevant word was spoken in twelve continuous hours of Indian programming. But the eleven and a half hours of Bollywood films and thirty minutes of star news had taken its toll on him.

Seated in front of his troops, the devoted soldiers of the Goddess, Ameer held a brass jug filled with water in one hand, and a yellow silk scarf in the other. Wrapped inside the silk cloth were three coins, one silver, and two copper, five pieces of turmeric, and the holiest of all ritual implements, the sacred pickaxe. A Thug was doomed to horrible, unspeakable punishments if he broke a vow sworn on the pickaxe. It was the tool of burial, and contained magic powers to ensure the sect's secrecy. Without stealth, they would cease to exist, brought to judgment by those who did not truly understand the ways of the Goddess. Secrecy itself was part of her divine plan.

"The pundit has said that we must go west for our next expedition," Ameer solemnly announced. The others murmured, "Hmmmm, West..." It was not entirely clear who "the pundit" was. Tradition demanded a brahmin priest, but how could they get one they could take into their confidence? It was not permitted to deceive one. Lying to the messenger to the Goddess might doom their enterprise to failure. Proof of pundit or not, the others took their leader's word. If Ameer said that the pundit wished them to go west, than they would go west. No questions asked. For his part, Ameer figured out the proper direction by spinning a cola bottle while intensely concentrating on the Goddess. Of course circumventing the priest by daring direct communication with the Divinity incurred a certain amount of risk, but he was confident that such infractions would be excused by his ardent devotion.

All sixteen devotees filed out of the live-work space and then walked across the nearly deserted street into a vacant lot. Ameer faced West, and with eyes raised to the heavens, he cried out, "Great Goddess! Universal Mother! If this our meditated expedition be fitting in thy sight, vouchsafe us help, and the signs of thy approbation!" With these holy words spoken, the men fell silent and waited for the Goddess's verdict. Without a good omen they could not go on.

"Eeeeeeeee-unnhhhhh! Eeeeeeeee-unnhhhhhh!" the ass brayed, from off to the right. The omen was good. The Goddess would take them by the right hand. (There wasn't really an ass in the lot. All members were perfect animal ventriloquists. It was a necessity. When they first began their holy work, they would endlessly wait for favorable omens. But they heard nothing. Now, they would draw secret lot, and the chosen one would make the appropriate sounds). "It is good! The omen is good!" Ameer declared. "Leave me in peace, my friends." The others went back across the street to wait for the call to leave, while their founder and leader meditated upon the Goddess for seven hours, as commanded by tradition. After he finished his deep reflections, they would set out towards the West to seek their victims. Direction, however, was largely ceremonial. They would take a few symbolic steps, and then pile into the mini-van. And today, they had a contract job.

Back in the warehouse space, a few of the Thugs went about their daily chores, scrubbing toilets, sweeping and mopping, or straightening up the place. A few others read to pass the time, having declined to join the gin-rummy game that was forming and which, as always, promised to turn into a seven-hour marathon tournament. This is when Ramesh liked his Thug comrades the best: relaxing, laughing. They were like any other group of guys passing the time. A club of good buddies, getting together to socialize and worship in their own way. And to murder helpless victims. Ramesh went to join the card game.

"Oh, Beloved Goddess, it is me, Harry, your faithful servant " Ameer always used his given name when addressing the Goddess. "I hope you will smile upon us again. It has been a good year, all things considered, and getting much better, despite this little situation. But with your help, Goddess, we will prevail through all the storms of life to reach great prosperity. She called us again today—it means more work, references, and then even more work! But she's a strange one. You must know. A very powerful yogini, ah, and very beautiful, but she lacks a proper balance. No sense of style, too brash. She's had a small taste of power, sweet as the *goor*, but doesn't understand what it can be—the power over life and death. How can her sex sprees compare to that? It is youth, is it not? She is unfit to fulfill Your great plan. But You have showed me the way! You have given me followers who see the beauty of these ancient ways. It was with Your hand, with I as your earthly instrument, that brought it all to life again! Oh Beloved Goddess, I see your face again! It is by your providence that we have attained our success. We have increased our revenues since we began taking contracts...sure, I put up a little fight before I accept them, but they would lose respect if I didn't. Such ignorance. But now we have a satellite dish, and I'm going to refurnish my office. We might all even take a little vacation together this year....they've been working –excuse me– so hard. I'm awfully sleepy, just can't stop yawning. I think I'll take a little catnap, and dream only of you, Divine One..."

ॐ

Having just left the Cafe Feu d'Amour, Aloysius walked down the street in his forceful, uncompromising stride, preoccupied even more than usual with thoughts of Phoebe. He neither looked where he was going, nor did he meet the eyes of the occasional passerby. She hadn't told him that she loved him in a long, long time. Had it been a month? It could have just been a week. It was whenever all these orgies started. He wouldn't go to one of them even if she asked him, and she never even asked him. But she was so damn beautiful. What could he do? And though he hadn't heard it in a long time, when she told him she loved him, it felt real. But they hadn't made love in a week. A long time for these two. The longest ever.

He had been lashing out a lot more at people. Yes, he was always angry, but it used to maintain itself at a medium simmer. Now, he was becoming dangerous to other people, and to himself. True, he didn't actually get thrown out of the Cafe. They would never do that. But the manager, a fat, mostly bald man, who sweat a great deal whatever the ambient temperature, did give him a significant look that said something like, "Get out until you learn to speak to my employees in a civilized manner." In response, Aloysius, angrily jeered, "Civilized! You call this place fucking civilized!" and then he knew it was time for him to leave. Apparently no one else had decoded the manager's silent message.

It was twilight. His favorite time. He cut across the street. Maybe they could work something out. Down the sidewalk. His pace increased with his optimism, tempered though it was. He had always found a way to adjust to Phoebe's needs. And, after all, she put up with him. Who else would? He needed her. All this sex was her means of salvation. Her yoga. He had to give her that. "This jealous boyfriend crap is stifling me," she told him. Shortcut, down the piss-smelling alleyway. She's had it tough. Growing up, moving around like that. Night had fallen. What was that? Lost in thought, he hadn't noticed the six men get out of the mini-van parked at the end of the alley. They walked up behind him, paced to overtake him, unconsciously keeping in step with one another.

Aloysius sensed them, and turned around suddenly, stopping them at a five foot distance. "What do you want?" he barked. He knew who they were. He had never actually seen them, but he knew. He knew where they came from, what they did, who their contacts were. When he first heard of the spate of stranglings and robberies ten years before he knew what was happening. The world of left-handed exported Indian religious cults was only so large.

"Perhaps you can help us find our way. We seem to be lost," replied one of the men, his line scripted long before. The others laughed.

"Lost is right. You know who I am? Don't you? You know my great yogic powers?"

"Of course we know who you are. That is why we are here," replied Ameer. He hadn't laughed at Aloysius. He had always respected him for his powers. If he had been capable of pity after the years of murder, he would have felt it for this victim more than any other.

"Tell me one thing..." Aloysius demanded. The men moved towards him and circled him. He made no move to flee. He would fight, but only when he knew it was hopeless. That despair would infuse him with the Anger he needed. "...Who sent you?"

"You know who sent us....Deep within your heart, you know who sent us. It is all for Her, you know. The Goddess."

"Bullshit."

"Bullshit? I don't think so, Mr. Aloysius Caine." Ameer took a long silk scarf from his pocket, wrapped each end around his hands, and pulled it taut.

Did Aloysius succumb to his suicidal urges and willingly offer his neck to the man with the silk? Surrender was not in his nature. He swore, he bit, he punched, he kicked. He was angry because he let himself be followed. He was angry because he trusted her and he was angry because she was letting this happen. And because he wasn't strong enough, and because he always knew it would end this way.

Aloysius was pinned to the ground. Two men held his legs, and two pressed down his shoulders. He still writhed and cursed. Just as Ameer came to wrap the scarf around his neck, the eight hands simultaneously released their grasp, shouting out in pain. Their hands had burned as if they had been held on a flame, as Aloysius's body heated to an inhuman level. "Goddamn motherfuckers! Let go of me you bastards!" Aloysius shouted. His body's temperature rose thousands of degrees a second. Blood and saliva, sputum and semen boiled within him. His skin bubbled and blackened and then his flesh burst out in flames. Smoke rose from his body, and he threw his head back and forth, his hair already a torch. In a moment it was over. Spontaneous combustion. Ashes, charred bones, and a set of perfectly preserved teeth connected to equally unscathed jawbones. Nothing else left.

"Most inauspicious!" Ameer whispered hoarsely. His men were too scared to speak, or to feel the pain of their burned hands. "Let us go. Very quickly!" They retreated down the alleyway and piled into the mini-van. Ameer gave an order to Ramesh, and he ran back to Aloysius' remains. More frightened that he had ever been before in his three years of being a Thuggee, Ramesh dropped the silk on Aloysius's ashes and ran back to his comrades. Ameer was scared. He had left the scarf out of respect for Aloysius, who had proved himself a great yogi today. But also, to deflect his displeasure with them. Driven by ambition, they had attacked a powerful holy man, stronger than he had imagined. He should have known. Surely their luck would turn worse now.

At precisely the same time that Aloysius met his fiery end, the manager of the Cafe Feu d'Amour was found face down in a puddle of his own urine in the Men's rest room. When he regained consciousness, his clothes damp from sweat and piss, his first words were "Fire, fire, everywhere!" Coincidence? Most probably. Such fainting spells, known by the clinical term "micturition syncopee" commonly afflict excessive perspirers, prone as they are to dehydration. But one man did take mental note of this incident, feeling that there was some extra-mundane reason for the manager's odd utterance. He was an attractive, well-dressed man in his mid-forties, his most

prominent, unusual feature being his dark, bushy eyebrow.
Singular. Eyebrow. What had been ordained to be two had
become one. And this was only the first hint of the feral
ferocity that lay beneath the well-primped exterior. He would
recall the manager's words in the not too distant future, when
news broke of a young man's death by burning. That there
was a connection was only a hunch, but his instincts had
served him well in his work for years. The hunch would soon
develop into a bona-fide clue when the dead man was identi-
fied by the coroner from a perfectly preserved, glistening set of
teeth. The discovery that the unfortunate young man was a
frequent visitor to the Cafe confirmed that indeed a psychic
connection with this particular criminal event had been
established.

After returning to the live-work space, Ameer bid his
followers to leave him alone, and shut himself in his office.
Four of the five Thugs who had witnessed Aloysius's fiery
ascent sought some sort of first-aid for their burns, which were
luckily only minor. The fifth, Ramesh, quickly spread the
news of the catastrophe to his comrades. The news was
depressing. The television was turned off, and the gin-rummy
game was immediately terminated. Each Thug sought out a
corner or closet or empty space along a wall to be alone with
his thoughts.

Aloysius's auto-cremation could only be a bad omen.
After emerging from the locker room, where medical supplies
were stored, the four injured Thugs each found their own
place to be alone.

Ameer picked up the phone, and punched in the numbers
so familiar to him the last couple of years. "He's dead, like
you asked. The angry one." He said nothing more, and hung
up the phone. How could he explain that Aloysius had burst
into flames?

She hung up the phone. Dead. Dead? "Like I asked?
What is he talking about?" Her stomach tightened, her head
whirled. She felt herself tumbling head over heels through an
unmitigated darkness, unable to stop or to get her bearings.

Down and down she fell, her arms and legs numb, useless. Determined to take hold of herself, she clenched her fists angrily, desperately trying to fight off the darkness. She could see just a small pinpoint of light. "He doesn't think that I wanted this to happen? Does he?" Nausea. And then complete darkness. But her plummet had suspended, and her body stayed perfectly still.

Tears welled up in her eyes and then spilled down her cheeks. She gasped to prevent a wail, but couldn't contain it. A wail emerged, and then a howl, and then a scream. She cried now without restraint. And the darkness began to recede. She felt her fingers again, her arms, her legs. Her body shook from sobs, and she shivered from a deep coldness. "Who ordered this?" she asked herself. Who could have done this? Was it her? Could she have? But she would never have done anything like this. She loved him. She loved him more than anyone else ever in her life. With all his faults, all his foolish jealousy, even his smoldering rage, she loved him. And she knew he loved her. The darkness began to recede. Her tears streamed down her cheeks. She stood feeling strong and sad, powerful and vulnerable.

"Who could have done this?" she wondered, her tears finally spent. "Why would anyone want to hurt him? What could be their reason?" Her moment of mourning passed, suspicions arose. Who could do such a thing? A traitor. It must have been a traitor. Someone close to her. Someone with knowledge of the secrets of the Order. Someone who knew of the Thugs. Someone who knew how to hurt her. Someone who wanted to destroy her happiness, to destroy all of her plans. To destroy her future. To steal what was rightfully hers. To steal her power.

"It must be Jacob."

9.

*T*wo weeks had passed since the discovery of Aloysius' remains and their positive identification. The only clue available thus far for the authorities was a yellow silk scarf found with the victim. And it would not have been a clue were it not for the insistent phone calls to the police department by a somewhat obsessive Indologist, Dr. Johannes Froese, who vehemently maintained that there was a connection to the murder of Ephraim Stockwell. But the police placed little faith in the good professor, though they had shared some information with him at first. Now the case had become a low priority, hidden deeply in the Unsolved Homicides file for lack of any clues other than those "discovered" by Professor Froese. It was a difficult case from the start. Witnesses had provided conflicting descriptions, "The club was dark," they all said. Memories failed. Were they afraid of retribution?

Meanwhile, Froese's continual phone calls did little but bring suspicion upon himself. The police began to look for evidence that Professor Froese and Ephraim Stockwell had been involved in an illicit love affair that had gone bad. Jealousy was always a motive for murder. Froese's career was flagging. Perhaps he was looking for a way to boost his fame with an elaborate conspiracy that only he could unravel. Maybe there was a three-way affair. Drugs may have been involved.

Yet not everyone involved with the case suspected Froese. Mortimer Aspen Finch knew quite a number of the detectives in the city police department in which he served before starting his own private investigation firm, Finch Inc. They tipped him off about their investigation of Froese, which Mortimer thought misguided. Mortimer relied upon his intuition for this judgment, rather than the fascination with vice and sleaze that had afflicted some of his former colleagues. He was famous amongst them for his flashes of intuition that would lead to the resolution of the most difficult of cases. Had he been born to a slightly later generation, his psychic abilities could have earned him a living on television, or as a 1-900 fortune-teller. His made-for-T.V. smile would have made him a natural. But he had followed a different way: first, as a successful police detective, and then as a renowned private detective.

When he first left the department, his dream had been to start his own private security company, hiring cops as security guards. He had looked forward to designing the uniforms for his employees, certain that the captains of business and indus-try would smile upon his vision of a smartly dressed, elite corp of fit, well-toned security professionals. But the guard-dog craze of the early part of the decade had put a damper on his entrepreneurial plans, and so he went into a far less glamorous profession. Less glamorous, that is, before he entered it. Mortimer brought a well-developed fashion consciousness wherever he went. He loved finely crafted Italian suits in such eyecatching colors as turquoise, magenta and sky-blue. And he had a love for silk scarves, which only heightened his interest in this particular murder case. His fashion decisions had gained almost as much attention as his intuition while he was in the department, though he nonetheless often felt underappreciated. He greeted one uniformed sergeant with upturned lip from the day he had made an inappropriate comment about Mortimer's "Eye-talian monkey suits" until he retired from the force. Such a violence he could never forgive. Nowadays, he would often meet prospective clients in riding breeches, with a riding crop tucked under his arm. Not actually an equestrian, Mortimer wore the outfit because he felt it lent him a continental aura.

Private Detective Finch put a call in to Professor Froese to get the details on his Thuggee theory. To Froese, there could be no doubt that Stockwell's strangulation by silk scarf was the work of Thugs. And as for the second fellow, Aloysius Caine, the scarf, exactly similar in size and color to that used on Stockwell, confirmed a connection. Froese, however, was troubled a bit by his theory. The Thuggees of India used to cut apart the bodies of their victim, and then bury them to hide any traces of their misdeeds. They did not leave silk scarves behind as calling cards. Secret cults were supposed to be secret. No one is supposed to know why they are, or what exactly they did.

In Stockwell's case, it was possible that the scarf was inadvertently left behind by the murderers in the rush to leave the club without being detected. Mistakes could always be made. But, Froese confided, the second scarf presented a more significant problem that could not be so easily explained away. Caine's murder –and Froese speculated that he been strangled first– was too much like the first to be a coincidence. The possibility that it was some kind of copycat crime was remote, since the dimensions of the first scarf were never mentioned publicly. It was very unlikely that these Thugs were so careless a second time as to forget another scarf. So, what happened? Why another scarf? And why did they incinerate their victim? The traditional Thuggees never did anything like that. Finch had a good feeling about the Professor's theory, and believed that the minor problems with it would be solved in due time. Responding to the Professor's doubts, he asked, "Who is to say that these Thugs still followed the old rules?"

Finch was so certain of the link between the deaths of Caine and Stockwell that he reported this theory to his employer, Dr. Nilesh Patel, director of the newly formed CPPILA. Hired to "clear up this nonsense as soon as possible," Finch's partiality to the Thuggee hypothesis was not appreciated by Dr. Patel. "There is no such thing as Thuggees, whatever this anti-Indian lunatic is saying!" he told Finch.

But Finch stood firm—he relied on his instincts; that was why he had a name in this business. He had spoken to Professor Froese himself. Lunatic he wasn't. Overzealous, yes. And he didn't know when to keep his mouth shut. But he wasn't crazy. "Find out who these phony Thugs are, then, Mr. Finch, with all your instincts and all your professors. We are paying you good money to put an end to this nonsense. I have to go. We're filming a commercial today!"

Mortimer had first come to the Cafe Feu d'Amour after the vague outlines of the Professor's speculation about cult activity had hit the papers, but before he had spoken to him. Word was out on the street that it was a hangout for members of various cults. In past years, these voices on the street never knew exactly who was in what cult, or for that matter, which cult was which, or even how many there, but they were certain that some kind of cult did exist. And that some of its members frequented the cafe. (These members were none other than Phoebe and Aloysius, though the Librarian would occasionally pop in to grab a double espresso to go). Also playing a role in convincing Finch that the Cafe might be a good place to hunt for clues were the Tantric recruiters pitching Phoebe's religious doctrines in the neighborhood. They were out in the open now, though they presented a sanitized version of cult activities and events. Phoebe was never mentioned by name, and cult members would never share their sworn secrets.

Now when Finch started going to the Cafe, he couldn't tell a Tantrika from a Thuggee, but he was only beginning to sort things out. He had noticed Aloysius before his death. He was hard to miss: an intense, apparently lonely man who elicited respect, or fear, from the staff and other regular customers. Once his death became common news at the Cafe, many patrons whispered of his probable affiliation with the Tantric Order that had made its presence public in recent weeks. Finch had all the more reason to visit the Cafe. If there was one cult connection to the place, why not another? Perhaps a rivalry over turf, or some kind of internal squabbling among fanatics.

Today, after days of uneventful coffee-sipping and surveillance of boring, clearly innocent cafe crowds, Finch was immediately struck by one of his flashes of intuition when a gorgeous, long black-haired woman came into the cafe. Her great beauty, and indeed her air of strength and resolution first provoked his interest, but he didn't know what her connection to his present case might be. But he knew that he wanted to keep his eye on her.

After Aloysius's flamboyant exit to the beyond, Phoebe had decided to patronize the cafe once again. At first, she only stopped by for a mocha to go, but this quick dash in-and-out grew into a pronounced loiter by the coffee bar after a couple of days. Soon, she was occupying a table, bringing her laptop, equipped with high resolution graphics, and her cellular phone. Staying for hours on end, she would speak in low whispers on the phone or design new group sexual positions with the aid of her computer. (She would quickly change screens when she felt curious eyes settle on her diagrams).

Why did she so brazenly seek a public place to do her very secretive work? She was conscious of the security risks, and she never worked on top secret matters while there. Her computer graphics work could always be explained away as "art"—a logo for a new company, or even a risque line of greeting cards. And she limited her cell phone calls to the most innocuous things: the reordering of gym mats, or condoms (in bulk). So, the high visibility was relatively low risk. Her motivation, then, could have been to revisit the place where Aloysius had spent so many hours, brooding, glaring at his coffee cups. Maybe some of his energy was still in the air, and she wanted to absorb more of it to ensure that her memories of him were eternal. She may have begun to frequent the cafe to prove her power: to show those who knew both him and her, and who perhaps had some vague notion of their true status, that she was not going to crumble after the death of her lover. She had the strength to continue, to live her life, to carry on her business. Or, perhaps it was because of both of these things. A love for Aloysius, and a need to demonstrate her strength. His death had changed little about her.

Phoebe did not come to the cafe alone. She was accompanied by a six foot five, three hundred pound muscle man and club bouncer who answered, with an "unh," to the name Dirk. She had exchanged phone numbers with him at the now infamous bhangra many weeks ago. Always looking for an energy-enhancing sexual encounter, she had quickly arranged a rendezvous while Aloysius's attention was focused elsewhere, bringing the behemoth into her unique world of tantra. She liked Dirk, finding his intellectual underachievement his most charming quality. Though she did think him a little too inflexible, due probably to his overindulgence in weightlifting. A yogi he would never be.

But Dirk was good for many things. For instance, he could carry in all of her groceries by himself, including the pounds upon pounds of ground beef that she required for left-handed sexual trysts. (It was not entirely clear whether Dirk enjoyed the beef-eating sacrament more than sex with Phoebe. He expressed his pleasure for both with an equal verbal agility and finesse). He was also quite good with furniture rearrangement. Phoebe insisted that her bedroom furniture be moved about so as not to bring up painful memories of Aloysius. Dirk obliged. Very soon, it became almost a daily occurrence. She liked to watch his muscles bulge, and his massive body perspire, and to hear him grunt as he lifted large objects. Burgers and sex followed soon afterwards.

While Phoebe sat in the cafe today, with her laptop computer and her cellular phone set on the table, someone was watching her. Dirk sat across from her, an adoring, stupid beast. Mortimer watched, taking mental notes, as his initial flash of intuition grew into a curious, suspicious force.

Jacob woke with a start. Another nightmare. One of two recurring dreams he had been having for the last several weeks. He sat up in his bed, remembering what he could. He knew what to expect, since the dream seemed to change little from night to night: Govind, untufted, ash-smeared Govind, danced around him, taunting him. "She doesn't like you anymore! She doesn't like you anymore!" he sang and then laughed wildly, his belly shaking back and forth. "She wants to kill you!" he jeered, and Jacob tried to shout, and then awoke. The dream had become a regular event, sharing air time with an older, equally frightening one, where Govind grabs Jacob by the foot and flings him into space, tearing him away from the wall of cubicles, and ending his ascent to a beautiful, radiant Phoebe standing above him. Determined now to stay awake, to prevent himself from dreaming such awful dreams again, Jacob sat up in bed, and reached for his pouch of tobacco. He had been getting very little sleep in the last week or two.

Since their fact-finding mission to the Library, Jacob and Sunita had been meeting regularly to exchange information, or really, to satiate Sunita's curiosity. She had done little reading on Tantra, and Jacob described his meetings with the Librarian and replayed the events leading up to the murder as best as he could, from his first experience with the mysterious Book, to his affair with Phoebe, to the strange occurrences on the day of the murder.

And each time Jacob reviewed the story, Sunita became convinced of one thing: Phoebe had plotted Jacob's murder. She wasn't sure why Phoebe would do such a thing, but all the data pointed in that direction. The most damning piece of evidence was Phoebe's reaction when she saw him alive and almost well in the street after the bhangra. Sunita speculated that the murderers had confused this poor Ephraim Stockwell fellow for Jacob. It would have been an easy enough mistake to make. It was dark, and if they had been hired, they may not have ever gotten a good look at their intended victim. (Whom Phoebe might have hired was never talked about.

That might have been one small detail that complicated their judgments). Jacob rejected the suggestion, and winced each time Sunita pressed her case. "It's obvious!" she would tell him, pleased with her detective skills, perhaps a little insensitive to Jacob's lingering feelings for Phoebe. He still loved her, he told Sunita, and he could not bring himself to believe that she could wish any harm to come to him. He finally countered Sunita's suggestion with his own, "Don't you see, Sunita, Aloysius put her up to it!" Now that was something Sunita hadn't considered. Perhaps she was too eager to find Phoebe guilty of some kind of heinous crime. "Maybe, Jacob, maybe. But it just doesn't seem right. It was her, Jacob. I truly think it was her. She really is capable of something like that." Strangely enough, their debate over Phoebe's guilt brought them closer together.

The next morning, after waking from another nightmare – they were now functioning as a no-batteries-required internal alarm clock– Jacob turned on the television set. Local news. Reporter Jack Flanagan was relating the story of the identification of a murder victim, Mr. Aloysius Caine, whose remains were found in an alleyway. Burned down to bones and ash. Jacob knew it had to be Phoebe. It was her. It was her all along. He picked up the telephone.

"Sunita?" he said weakly, barely able to say her name.

"Yeah...Who is this? Jacob? Do you know what time it is?" He didn't answer. "Jacob? What's wrong? Did something happen?"

"She killed Aloysius, Sunita. She killed him. It was her. It had to be her."

"I'll be right over."

"I'm doing this because he's a good friend," she assured herself on her way over to Jacob's apartment. They were getting close, and he needed someone right now. He needed her. She knew what if felt like to have somebody you believed in –somebody you needed to believe in– turn out not to be what you thought they were. Yes, she was going to be a good friend to him. But wasn't it odd how quickly she felt the need to comfort him? "Oh, Sunita! You know he needs a friend right now." That was all. But she doesn't rush out the door like this for anyone, except family...And Tex, she would definitely speed out the door if Tex needed her...she is there for her friends, and Jacob is a friend. A good friend.

It was quite painful to recognize that the woman he had loved for two months had plotted to kill him. Though Jacob had grown quite used to not having Phoebe in his life. His love and what he saw as his unchallengeable faith in her had been sustained mostly out of habit in this last month. The reason? Although not yet acknowledged, passionate love and longing had cooled to empty, ritualistic proclamations of "I love her" because of a quickly ripening desire for Sunita.

But of course, the realization of Phoebe's guilt did take an emotional toll on Jacob. How often does one discover that the woman to whom you have given up your not-so-precious male virginity hired someone to strangle you at a nightclub?

In the time it took for Sunita to get to his apartment, Jacob had cleaned himself up, and set a pot of coffee to brew. When she arrived downstairs, he buzzed her into his building and waited for her at the front door. She followed him into his euro-kitchen ("euro" being a euphemism for "unable to contain more than two adults at the same time"). Jacob turned to her and said "Sunita, I feel so alone right now...Just hold me." She obliged.

"I guess it's true. You were right all along," he murmured, still hugging her. It was quite a pleasant embrace for them both, and neither seemed particularly willing to decouple, nor even surprised that the other hadn't tried to already.

"That doesn't matter, Jacob. You're o.k. That's the most important thing. And you're going to get through this whole thing. You will weather this, Jacob. I have faith in you. She's sick, you know...." She pulled her face back so that she could look into his eyes. "I've been so worried about you...." And then, she kissed him. On the cheek. A slight peck. Actually, less than a peck, but much more than an air-kiss launched in the vicinity of a proffered cheek.

And then he kissed her. A tongue-less sliding of the lips. Coffee continued to percolate and bubble on the white-tile counter. Nicodemus interrupted his self-cleaning, tongue at mid-stomach, and took a moment to observe.

Tongues fluttered and wrestled. Lips puckered and smacked. Several weeks worth of repressed energy sought release, though no magical aura of light surrounded them. Each drew the other closer. Necks were kissed, ear lobes were nibbled. Genitals self-lubricated, independently celebrating the First Make-Out Session.

Jacob took Sunita's hand in his and led her to the couch. He unbuttoned her shirt, pulling her bra down to at last allow her nipples oxygen. He brought mouth and wiggly tongue on one and then the other....

"Jacob," she whispered, "sto-op."

"Stop?" he asked, while continuing to fondle her breasts, and even more excited by the way she said his name.

"Stop," she said firmly. He lifted his head, and looked into her eyes, pleading. She raised an eyebrow.

"Stopped. Done." He pulled away from her, untensed his muscles and took a deep breath. Sunita lifted her bra to cover herself, and buttoned her shirt. "What's wrong, Sunita?"

"I can't do this—"

"What's the matter?"

"I told you once before. You know why."

"But Sunita, it's not about that. It's about you and me...."

"That's exactly it...this is me. This is a part of me. Part of me really wants to be with you. You know that. But it can't be that way. I made a promise to myself."

"You can break that promise. You said so yourself—you want to be with me."

"Jacob, only a part of me wants you, but there are other parts to me. And they tell me that this is wrong. That this will only lead to something where I have to deny myself. Just look at this whole thing, Jacob. Get some distance."

"Sunita, I have thought about this....And I've thought about us. I know what you've been through, and I'm not going to let that happen. I won't stop you from being who you are."

"How do you know who I am?"

"That's not fair! You're an Indian woman, but you're also Sunita Chidha—, Sunita Chid-um-bar-um. An individual. My friend. And I want you to be my lover. Is that such a bad thing?"

"Look at yourself Jacob! You say you can handle this, but it's not something to handle! It's a whole way of seeing things, a way of being. I don't know if it's possible for you to understand. The whole multicultural talk is just that—a bunch of pony-tailed liberal men ooh-ing and ah-ing about how sensitive they are. And if that self-congratulatory garbage isn't bad enough, they end up idealizing and worshiping all this mysterious knowledge of the East. You're damn straight, Jacob, I'm an exotic beauty, but it's not for you!...I'm sick of it all. Either no one ever pays attention to me, or all of a sudden I'm a prize to be had, or I fulfill some white man's fantasy of the Orient. I'm sick of it, and I'm going to fight back!"

"Sunita, all you are is angry right now. It's nothing but anger," he said slowly.

"You're damn right I'm angry! Three hundred years of colonial oppression –who knows how many years of indigenous patriarchal power– and now, here we are in America, and we're either laughed at for our accents and the way we dress, or we're invisible. And every white man here wants to save me from my parents!"

"I understand your anger—"

"No, you don't understand. That's the whole point—"

"—but, it will only burn you up."

At home that night, Sunita received an unexpected phone call. "Vikram? Vikram is that you?" she excitedly responded to his nearly whispered "Hey Sunita."

"Yeah, it's me."

"It's been awhile, huh....." she offered in reconciliation.

"Yeah, it has. I guess you've been too busy to call me— "

"You know how it is. I guess I've had a lot on my mind."

—Busy with this Jacob guy."

"What do you mean by that?"

"Can't find the time to call me, but you've got plenty of time for him.....I don't understand what your problem is, Sunita. You go around making a big deal about this kind of thing, and then there you go, the first chance you get, you throw yourself at this guy!"

"I did not throw myself at anyone, Vikram!"

"And what happened to me? I've known you for a long, long time, Sunita, and now I don't matter at all. It's like all of a sudden you're pretending you don't even know me—you are just so spoiled Sunita –spoiled– that's what you are!"

When Vikram was sufficiently berated by an enraged Sunita –he stood accused of sexism, racism, and homophobia for good measure– the phone was slammed down. It remained at rest for approximately twelve seconds, in which time Sunita began to process the question, "How did he of all people know about Jacob?" She felt justified in her anger toward Vikram the Meddler, especially since he presumed a far greater romantic status than was his due. But she also felt a strange pang of guilt. Maybe she did abandon him....The guilt made her angrier. "Tex! It was Tex! The double-crossing little shit!" Sunita punched in digits with a forceful precision.

"Howdy," Tex answered.

"Look here, you redneck sonofabitch—where do you get off spreading my business around?"

"Sunita?"

"Who else would it be? Or are you spreading rumors about more than one woman this week?"

"Sunita, what are you talking about?" He knew.. He knew he would be found out, he was certain he would be branded a traitor, called names, insulted for his deed. Ignorance seemed a wise stalling tactic, until a better defense could be formulated.

"I'm talking about all this stuff you've been telling Vikram. He thinks I've been spending every second of the day with Jacob. Like I'm in love or something! What business is it of his anyway? Who the hell does he think he is? And who the hell do you think you are with all your self-righteous crap?"

"Did Vikram tell you that I told him about you and Jacob?" Admit nothing, yet.

"No. I figured it out. Who else is going to be sticking his not-so-small-nose into my business but you? And what's all this 'you and Jacob' talk. There is no 'me and Jacob.' He's a friend, Anil, a friend."

Tex quickly realized the depth of Sunita's fury when she called him by his given name. He had to outmaneuver her, to go on the offensive. It would be for her own good. "You've been spending a lot of time with him, Sunita. A lot of time. You don't seem to have time for your other friends. Do you even realize that? What's so great about him, Sunita? Are you so impressed by all his new age-tantra-yoga-garbage? He's more of a Hindu than you! God, Sunita. He's got a fetish, and you're eating up the attention!'

"What's that supposed to mean?"

"You love getting all that attention from them—"

"What are you talking about? Are you going to go find me a 'nice Indian boy' now?"

"Maybe it wouldn't be such a bad idea, Sunita. You seem to have forgotten who you are and where you come from."

"Thanks, Tex. You should be the one to remind me where I come from, Tex. Hmm, 'Tex', is that Punjabi or Hindi for hypocrite?"

Ear still ringing from Sunita's slamming down of the phone, Tex took a moment to think over his predicament. What was he going to do? Or, really, whose side was he going to choose, since sides were going to have to be chosen. Vikram had already threatened Tex with bodily harm should he fail to report all he knew about Sunita's burgeoning relationship with Jacob. "If you don't keep me informed, Tex, I'll make *vindaloo* of you," he said. Was it an idle threat? Hard to say, though it was often spoken by Vikram, who knew his Hindi from Indian restaurant menus and the occasional Bollywood film. From these he would mine a suitable phrase or word or two, and string them together to make nearly coherent sentences that gave him an air of ethnic authenticity. In most circumstances, that image rendered him an ominous figure—an unknown threat, an Other who was to be feared. The hapless Occidental could only wonder at what severe indignities, not to mention horrible pain, that one must suffer through to be made into vindaloo. And for those who may themselves frequent the same Indian dining establishments as Vikram, the threat was no less: after all, what terrible tortures, only now concealed under a seemingly innocent culinary description, had the East Indian imagination concocted centuries ago and named "vindaloo"? Tex, of course, new the true meaning of the term, not to mention its means of entering Vikram's lexicon. In this case, Tex did not fear the Unknown, but rather, the very known quantity of Vikram's temper, which had not ever erupted into violence as far as Tex knew, but which was to be feared nonetheless, for it could lead to a premature severing of a friendship that Tex did value. But he also knew what Sunita's reaction might be if she were to find out about his "sharing" of information about she and Jacob. It was a bad position to be in. He knew that Jacob wasn't right for her. And though she may never come knocking on his doors with love in her eyes and a fiery passion in her loins –that possibility being precluded by his tobacco chewing habits– he could at least keep an eye on her....and keep her away from Jacob. And Vikram was not such a bad guy.... *"Hum bane, tum bane ek duje ke liye*....tell her I said that, just like that," he had told Tex. (Something else he had picked up from a film). For all his clumsiness, Tex knew that Vikram really felt something for her. It would be better if they were the ones to see each other...They would look so good together...

10.

At the Cafe Feu d'Amour, Mortimer Finch sat at his table, a frothy double cappucino before him. He was here to watch Phoebe, who had not arrived yet, convinced that she must know something about Mr. Caine's death. And if that were the case, she might also have had a hand in the murder of Mr. Stockwell. Finch's intuition had made itself known stronger than ever before. This time, he had a dream in which Phoebe, whom he had kept under surveillance for so many hours, made a guest appearance. His was not directed fantasy or lascivious daydream, but an all senses engaged, deep-sleep dream. Beautiful Phoebe, a gem in her navel, performed a belly dance for Sheik Mortimer Finch. She shook the bells on her bangles, as she leaned towards the sheik, granting him a vision of her cleavage. She straightened, and began to spin about. Every time she faced him, she lay an exquisite silk at his feet, each a different color. Upon touching the ground, the red, purple silver or green silk turned yellow, golden yellow, now the color of death.

When Finch remembered his dream in the morning, he was certain that he knew that Phoebe was responsible. Since he couldn't ever tell anyone his dream –it would be too much even for the admirers of the great Mortimer Finch– he had to gather evidence, observing the murderess, waiting for her to slip up and reveal her guilt. Today, he would wait for her, wait until she came in to the cafe, just as she always had for weeks. He would wait, patiently and watch now that he knew it was her.

Jacob lay in bed, eyes fixed on the television. The program? A thirty minute infomercial sponsored by a group of
well-meaning leaders of the Indian-American community (or
was it Indo-American? They couldn't seem to decide what to
call themselves during the program). "India, land of the Taj
Mahal. Land of exotic beauty. Land of great diversity..."
lectured the announcer, melodramatically. Pictures of dancers,
temple statues Bombay high rises, Bangalore condominiums
and Tata trucks flashed by rapidly. "The great Kipling was
mistaken. "East and West, never shall the twain meet,' said the
poet. But meet they have, in the land called America." Cut to
Statue of Liberty, to the sounds of free-jam raga. Music fades
to patriotic sound, accomplishment-oriented light rock, heard
usually during commercials for technical schools. Shot of
Indian doctor meeting with patients, men and nose-pierced
women with lab coats looking into microscopes, smiling.
"Indian-Americans have made great contributions in the field
of medicine." Series of graphs and charts plotting the number
of physicians of Indian descent by medical specialty. "Indians
are also leaders in the technical fields." Cut to wide pan of
Silicon Valley. Bespectacled Indians in casual-wear walking
around on campus of large high technology firm. "Pursuing
the American dream, Indians have succeeded in the land of
their adoption." Close with the appearance of a Congressman
from a not-so-obscure Western state, courting Indo-dollars –
party affiliation unimportant so long as there is participation–
"Our great nation has a lot to gain from our Indian immigrants and Indian-American citizens. They have proved
themselves to be leaders in medicine, technology and business.
It is with their help, and their presence in this great nation of
immigrants that our great country will meet the challenges of
the twenty-first century. I have many personal friends who are
Indian-Americans. And I remember thinking once, over a
shared meal of their native dish, called 'curry,' that we are not
so different from our Indian friends. We both love America
and the opportunities it provides."

Jacob turned off the television. Sunita had been on his mind for all of the day before, and through the night, causing him to toss and turn in his sleep. He was beginning to feel guilty —as if he had abandoned Phoebe– but would he have felt this way if Sunita and he were to have made love?—and guilty because he could not be what Sunita seemed to want him to be, even though he didn't know what that was. Such confusion, torn between Sunita and Phoebe, when he thought so much had already been settled. But how foolish of him to think that everything could have reached such a point of calm—emotions could never subside so quickly, so effortlessly. He had forgotten all that his guru had taught him. Where was his control? But he had given up on the path even before he began. Falling in love with Phoebe was not something he was supposed to do. What turned her so against him? How could she hate him the way Sunita made him believe she did? Maybe Sunita was wrong. Ah, Sunita. So beautiful, so kind, so strong.

"Oh, my guru, how desperately I need your guidance sometimes, though I have never lived up to your great example," he said aloud, before beginning his meditations. He focused upon the image of his teacher, trying to empty his mind of Phoebe and Sunita, ridding himself of his worries and fears so that he might consult his master to find the best way to attend to these newest complications. Jacob could hear his voice as clearly as if he were alive; he felt his presence. The old man lived on. "Could Phoebe really have wanted to hurt me? Would Sunita overcome her fears? Whom do I truly love?" he asked. What answer did he receive? "Remember, Jacob, you were the one who was chosen." But what is to become of Phoebe?

Jacob's musings were interrupted by the shrill ring of his practically antique telephone. He guessed Sunita. He was wrong. "Jacob? It's Phoebe."

"Phoebe? How are you?" he asked, pleasantly, but with effort. Stomach churned, neck muscles pinched in alarm.

"I'm pretty good. I'm sorry I haven't called in such a long time. I've really needed some time. You have every right in the world to hang up right now. But I hope you won't."

"I won't hang up. I'm listening."

"You heard about Aloysius?"

"Yeah." He tried to detect the faintest hint of guilt, but to no avail.

"It's absolutely awful. He's been on my mind all the time. I mean, after he asked me back again that night at the club— you know, when we saw you, I didn't know what you were thinking. I just didn't know what to say. He just kept going on that night about how good we were together. And you were acting so strangely."

"Phoebe, you threw me out that day!"

"What else could I have done Jacob? Aloysius was practically knocking the door down. He has –had– quite a temper. It made him so many enemies. I always feared something like this would happen. He was so passionate, but he had no control of himself. Now someone has destroyed him. There's nothing left....nothing..." she whispered and sobbed softly.

"Phoebe, don't, please."

"He just couldn't let go, and he couldn't face the fact that you and me were together...Both of you left me that night..."

Two, no, three people heard and believed what Phoebe said. The first was Phoebe herself, who knew that there was a basic truth to what she said. They both did leave that night in a sense. And it was true that Aloysius couldn't accept that she had been seeing Jacob. Aloysius also had made enemies whether he chose to or not. The second to believe was Jacob. Whatever he or Sunita had said, he did still care deeply for Phoebe. It wasn't love anymore, but it was something. And what she said made sense. He had been too quick to jump to all sorts of conclusions, from questioning Phoebe's loyalty to thinking that she was capable of murder. Aloysius was a tough character, and he didn't know very much about him. He scared Jacob the first time they met, and he probably scared others as well. People combat their fear by striking out, so it was inevitable that someone lashed out at Aloysius. Phoebe needed him now, and if she was lying—but she wasn't, couldn't have been. He would have been able to tell: they were together for two months, two whole months, every single day. He could at least tell if she was telling the truth when he spoke to her.

The third to hear and believe? A large, hulking man, almost brought to tears when Phoebe said, "You both left me that night." Hardly a sensitive one, even he could feel her sense of abandonment and her profound aloneness, which were more true than the truth of any single sequence of events, and more true than any one night of misunderstandings and petty betrayals. Dirk was moved to say the most caring thing he had ever said in his life, "I won't leave you, Phoebe. That sonofabitch will pay for what he did to you."

"Let me work on one failed attempt at love at a time, " Jacob had told Sunita, when she asked to see him today, to talk about the day before. He was adamant when she warned him not to meet Phoebe. "She's up to no good. What did she say to you?"

"Look, Sunita, I'll tell you later. But I've already made up my mind to speak to her—"

"I want to talk to you. Before you go. Now."

"Sunita, I can take care of myself. I'm going to meet her now, anyway. Just to talk. It's not a big deal."

"Of course it's a big deal. For all we know, she's a murderer. What happened to all that you said yesterday? I'm going to call the police."

"And tell them what, some woman's jilted boyfriend thinks that she's a deranged serial killer. 'Evidence, officer? Oh, yes, well my friend and I have a really strong feeling about this one.' Come on, Sunita, we'd make fools of ourselves. And to tell you the truth, I really don't think she's involved in all of this. I feel kind of bad for even thinking that she was..."

"Just wait for me there. I'm on my way."

"No, Sunita. I'm out of here now. I've got to meet her in half an hour."

"Jacob, if you go and do this and get yourself killed, I will not forgive you."

"I'll be fine."

"Where are you meeting her?"

"Goodbye, Sunita. I'll tell you about everything later, over a cup of coffee."

After Jacob hung up the phone, Sunita called Tex. Jacob wasn't thinking clearly, and she would just have to ignore his request. "Oh, Sunita. How nice of you to call the hypocrite...."

"Come on, Tex, we'll talk about that later. I think Jacob's about to get himself in some big trouble. I need your help. Can you come get me?"

"My brother's in town, and he's temporarily repossessed his pickup. He's out scouting sites for a new branch for his urine therapy company. Sunita, he wants to put an advertising placard on the truck! He'll ruin me."

"Tex! This is a life and death matter we're talking here! I'll take a taxi and come get you."

Settled in the cab, Sunita nervously tapped her fingers on the back door armrest. "Hello, Miss," said the driver.

"Hello," replied Sunita, preoccupied, and a little unwilling to talk.

"Are you Indian?"

"Yes I am. Well, I was born here, but my parents are from India."

"I'm from Pakistan. India and Pakistan—makes no difference here. Don't you think Miss."

"Right. Really makes no difference to me. We're all the same people."

"You are absolutely right, Miss. Do you like Hindi music?"

"Sure." The driver selected a tune that sounded familiar to Sunita, but she didn't know the name of it. It did make her smile though. A little more relaxed, she took a better look at the decor of the cab—and it was worthy of closer examination. White fuzzy carpet on the dashboard. A row of mirrors, six in all, extended from the driver's side sun visor all the way across to the passenger side. Compact disc player connected to eight speakers distributed in key positions throughout the cab, and, judging from the vibrations in the backseat, to a subwoofer also.

Sunita inspected the cabbie's picture ID card. It must have been an old photo, so little did it resemble him. Perhaps one taken in Pakistan, Sunita imagined. But the real man looked so much younger than his photo. He lacked any hint of a beard, though he did have a thin mustache, grown for syle, or perhaps, as a bold proclamation, "Yes, hair can be grown upon this face!" And on his head there was much more hair now than when the photo was taken: proudly uncombed, passionate, wavy hair.

"Your name is Afziz? Afziz Ahmed?"

"Yes. Afziz. Well, no. My brother is Afziz. I am driving his cab today. It is very illegal. If the policeman comes, I will say only 'No English, no English."

"Good plan."

"We have just made our cab very nice. Do you like it?"

"Oh, yes. Absolutely. It's wonderful. Really very comfortable."

"Do you have a television?"

"A television? Yeah. But I don't watch it much."

"Have you seen this new commercial, Miss? This one that shows all of these *Desis* on the television—all of them doctors and engineers, all wealthy men. I was saying to my brother Afziz, 'Afziz, brother, what do you think of all of this? All of these rich fellows on the television.' And my brother said to me, 'Aijaz, my brother, I think it is a sad day for all of us. Now everyone in America thinks we are rich fellows. Where is our money? No, Aijaz, my brother, it is a sad day. Now enough of this nonsense, let us see this new video—I'm getting ready to dance.' He is such a good dancer, my brother.

Not me, I am best when I am watching. How about you,
Miss?....Miss, Miss, have you seen this commercial?"

Before Sunita could answer, the cab pulled up in front of
Tex's apartment building. She got out to ring Tex. She hadn't
seen the commercial, but she really had been listening to Aijaz,
fascinated, quickly imagining his home with Afziz and who
knows how many others. Tex came down, and he and Sunita
got in the waiting taxi. She called out the address for the Cafe
Feu d'Amour.

"Where are we going, anyway, Sunita?"

"Jacob is meeting Phoebe somewhere, and I don't trust her
with him."

"Right, I've heard your theory," Tex replied, with a hint of
condescension. Sunita noticed, but let it pass, without deign-
ing to shoot an "indulge me" glance. "Would they have to
spend the cab ride in a game of unspoken one-upmanship?"
she wondered. She wasn't in the mood for it, but she would
fight back.

"So where are they meeting?" Tex didn't want to hear the
theory again, let alone argue. It would be easier to let Sunita
think she was getting her way. And they could stop for a bite
to eat afterwards, where she could apologize profusely. He
would, of course, forgive her when she did. That's the kind of
person he was, he assured himself. He was big enough, too,
not to bring it up while they drove around looking for Jacob
and his psychotic ex-girlfriend.

"I'm not sure—('it's good to see him back down' she
thought). But I figure there's three possible places that they
might be..." Tex felt to see if he brought his wallet –he would
insist on paying– as Sunita continued. "...her apartment, that
cafe Jacob told us about, and the Library. I have no idea where
she lives, and I'd bet you a hundred bucks her number is
unlisted. So, we'll check the other two. The cafe first, since it
will be much faster to look there."

"Right. Hey, Sunita, it will all turn out O.K."

"Listen, Tex. About last night...." Aijaz looked in the first
mirror into the back seat, waiting to hear what Sunita would

say next. "...let's just forget about it. We both said some things..." It wasn't quite the apology he had hoped for, but Tex was satisfied. It was the closest thing to one Sunita would offer. Besides, he wasn't a demanding man.

"Hey, it's O.K. Sunita," Tex replied, and put a friendly hand on her right thigh. Aijaz's eyebrows jumped up, and then he quickly began to monitor the back seat action in the second mirror, and then the third and forth, to make sure what he thought was happening was actually happening. He couldn't check the fifth and sixth since they were for show only. "Aijaz has told me about this kind of thing, and now it has happened only my second time," he thought. Sunita held Tex's hand. Aijaz fumbled with the CD player and punched in the number for the most moving love song on the disc, the kind of song that brought Bollywood stars to the Himalayas, where men could strike manly poses, and women could run with dupatta flowing majestically, suggestively.

"Tex you have to understand something about Jacob. I don't love him. I care very deeply for him, but I don't love him." Aijaz began to shake.

"If you say so, Sunita. I guess I just don't want anything to happen to you. You're too close to me for that."

"Thanks Tex. And I think Tex is a wonderful nickname," Sunita said and laughed.

"You know, Sunita —and please don't get angry— Vikram might have a little bit of a point. Ya'll have been spending a lot of time together, and you seem to care for him an awful lot. It's just strange, Sunita, you wanted to change so many things about yourself after Thaddeus..."

"I did. I did change so much, Tex, you're right. I learned so many things about myself and who I am and where I come from. Things I was never allowed to explore before. But I can't hate them, Tex. I can't hate people —it's not even a question of hate— I just can't shut people out."

"You can't lose yourself either...Seems like that's the hardest choice."

"So am I the real me when I'm around a bunch of Indians? How close do I have to be when the real Sunita pops up, ten feet, five, or do I have to be sleeping with one?"

"I don't know, Sunita....But what about us?"

"Here we are, Miss," said Aijaz, quickly turning around to make sure that everyone had remained modest, but hoping that they hadn't.

"I'll be right back, Tex. I don't think they're here. But I'll ask someone if they've seen her. Aijaz, could you hold the cab? I'll be back in a minute."

"Of course, Miss."

Sunita turned quite a few heads when she walked into the Cafe. One head in particular, belonging to Mortimer Finch, responded to a surge of intuitive electricity, and involuntarily jerked to the left to watch the long-haired, dark-skinned beauty. She stood at the doorway, squinting her eyes because of the smoke while she scanned the faces of the cafe patrons. Finch's single eyebrow arched up, revealing his interest in the young woman as both criminologist and as lecherous middle-aged heterosexual male. Sunita realized that she was already being far too conspicuous by remaining at the doorway for so long. She had formulated a response just in case Jacob was actually in the cafe. Were he there, he would be angry at her meddling; she would simply tell him, "You told me about the place. I had some free time and just wanted to check it out." Besides, if Phoebe were planning something, Sunita wanted her to know that she was there. That way, nothing would happen to Jacob.

She slowly made her way through the cafe and up to the coffee bar, behind which sat a man on a stool, sweating profusely for no apparent reason. He looked worried, though he managed to smile at Sunita. "Can I help you?" he asked, and gulped a glass of water in three swallows. He seemed to sweat the entire contents of the glass immediately upon finishing.

"Yes, I'm looking for someone. She comes in fairly often, I think. Phoebe Keli is her name. You can't miss her—really striking, long black hair, very fair skin."

"I know Phoebe. She hasn't been here all day." The manager poured himself another glass of water and drank it as quickly as the first. He continued to sweat.

"I'm also looking for a guy. He's got kind of messy brown hair. He's thin, kind of cute. His name is Jacob. Have you seen him?"

"Naw, doesn't sound familiar. You'll have to excuse me, ma'am, I'm feeling a little faint." He rose and slowly walked in the direction of the men's room. Sunita turned around and caught sight of the moldings on the ceiling. Erotic temple sculptures. "Damned orientalists," she thought. She pursed her lips and angrily strode through the cafe and out the door. Finch watched the entire encounter though he could hear nothing of it. He himself had been waiting for Phoebe, but she hadn't shown up at what was now her usual time.

When Sunita got back in the cab, she responded to both Aijaz and Tex's inquiring looks by shaking her head. A bored Tex had more or less filled in Aijaz on Sunita's rescue mission and search for Jacob. A sympathetic man, Aijaz had immediately made up his mind not to charge the distressed heroine in her moment of need. To seal the deal for the zero fare, Tex let it slip that Sunita had loved he himself dearly once, but his family had forbidden the union—regional differences, and well, she was too dark. Their love had been denied. Upon hearing yet another twist in this tale of woe, Aijaz began to feel that he was playing a small but pivotal role in a Hindi film come to life. "Afziz, my brother," Aijaz imagined himself later saying, "it had to be this way. She was a beautiful young woman in need, and I did what any man would do. And I tell you, my brother, I think that if I had stayed with them a little longer that afternoon, that lotus flower would have shown her radiant smile to me. But she is a Hindu, and I am a Muslim, and I knew our beloved father would not have given his blessings for such a union. Who knows what her parents would have said? I have heard stories of parents killing their daughter's beloved for the sake of religion. It is a difficult world when such things will keep two people in love from marrying one another and having six children, like our beloved father did with our beloved mother."

Sunita turned to Tex, "We've got to get to the Library. And quick! Aijaz! Aijaz..."

"Yes miss," Aijaz dreamily responded.

"We need to get somewhere fast! Really fast..."

"No problem. No problem...."

After getting off the phone with Sunita, Jacob hurriedly primped himself and rushed out the door. He was more excited than he would have liked to admit. When he reached the Library, he headed directly to the Hall of Cubicles cum Orgy Room. The gymnasium mats and industrial fans, turned off now, remained in place in the faintly lit hall, but Phoebe wasn't waiting there like she said she would be. The hall seemed empty, even of the ubiquitous Govind. Jacob made himself comfortable, sitting cross-legged in the center of the mats. Phoebe could be running a little late...After a few minutes, Jacob heard footsteps from behind him. He tensed up—they were much, much too heavy to be Phoebe's.

"Phoebe?" he called, without turning around, desperately hoping that it would be she who answered.

"No, you little shit. It's not Phoebe."

Jacob recognized the voice, but he didn't know from where. Aloysius? But that was impossible. He slowly stood up and turned around. Jacob couldn't see the man's face, but his body was tremendous. Huge. Muscular. He got closer and closer to Jacob. He was carrying a rope.

"You're that bouncer from the club. Aren't you?" Jacob finally recognized him, when he was only a few steps away.

"That's right. Do you know what I'm going to do to you, you little shit?"

"Well –I– hey what the hell are you doing?" Dirk had lunged at Jacob, and he fell limply under three hundred pounds of flesh. Within a minute, Jacob was hogtied and squirming, while Dirk stood over him. "What the hell is this! Where is Phoebe?"

"You've got a lot of nerve asking about Phoebe, you little shit. Haven't you hurt her enough already?"

"What are you talking about?"

"Shut up! Shut up!" Dirk shouted, enraged, his face red, specks of saliva flying from his mouth.

Jacob thought it a wise survival tactic to say nothing. After his outburst, the entire hall was silent, except for the sound of Dirk's heavy breathing. Several minutes passed. Jacob lamented the fact that he never took that self-defense elective before dropping out of divinity school. Dirk held his breath. He was listening for something. "There it is again," he finally said. "It better not be that little naked guy. Govind? Is that you? Get out of here..."

"All right, then, I'm going to come get you."

Dirk headed toward one of the back passageways. He intended to restore order in the Hall of Cubicles, for that was what he had always been called upon to do—to control, to manage, to contain the irregular to ensure the smooth operation of events. He was, after all, a bouncer. Dirk took his station quite seriously. Something of a neo-imperialist in temperament, his method of reestablishing harmony consisted of picking up objects smaller than he and placing them down again somewhat violently. He intended to do this with Govind, whom he believed to be lurking about, and he planned to do this with Jacob. Only he would not be placing him down upon dry land.

Aijaz had begun to take his role in this developing melodrama very seriously. He swerved his taxi in and out of traffic on his way to the Library. Tex and Sunita were lurched from side to side, and held on tightly to the door handles for support. In keeping with the high drama of the moment, Aijaz had selected a particularly heroic song culled from his brother's collection of Hindi film songs. Sunita's fear for

Jacob's safety subsided a bit. Somehow Aijaz's zealousness had lessened her own conviction that she was foiling an intricate crime plot.

"I am knowing a shortcut Miss," Aijaz cried out as he turned down an alley. He sat up straight in his seat with his chest pushed out, and his nostrils flared. Finally pulling up in front of the Library, Aijaz turned down the volume enough for dialogue to take place, and announced, "We are here!"

"Thank you, Aijaz," said Sunita. He looked over his shoulder and grinned. "How much do we owe you?"

"Oh, no. It is nothing."

"No, let me pay you something." She held out a twenty.

"Please, Miss, I cannot accept any money from you," he replied, waving the bill away. "Please, I cannot take this..."

Sunita didn't want to argue, since it might be ungracious to refuse his offer. As she climbed out of the taxi, Aijaz called out to her, "I hope you find your boyfriend, Miss. And remember my name, Afziz 'Cowboy' Ahmed. 'Cowboy' is my nickname. Good luck to you." He waited until Sunita and Tex walked up the stairs and passed through the doors before pulling away.

Tex was a few steps behind Sunita as she led the way into the inner recesses of the building and through the intricate maze that held the headquarters of the tantric cult. When they finally reached the edge of the "Great Sex Hall," as Tex termed it, Sunita stopped suddenly. A body lay inert on the gym mat, about twenty feet away in the center of the dimly lit hall. It could very well have been a sleeping Govind, but Sunita feared the worst. "It's Jacob," she thought. "We're too late." Tex caught up with her and came to her side, taking a moment to catch his breath. When he saw the body, he knew what she was thinking. "We can't be sure," he said aloud. His voice echoed through the entire hall, reverberated into each of the cubicles and then finally bounced back past them and down the hallway from which they came.

When he heard Tex's voice, Jacob rolled over as best as he could. "Psst," he signaled, letting them know that there was still life in his tired and bruised body, but also that silence must be maintained because danger was near. Dirk had just left seconds ago to investigate the sounds in the shadows, ready to discipline Govind for his disobedience.

Relieved, Tex and Sunita managed a tip-toe run across the hall to Jacob. "Be quiet," Jacob mouthed, as his rescuers rolled him over to untie his hands. Tex then lifted his torso up so Sunita could unravel each successive loop of rope from around his body. Jacob lifted his own legs while Sunita loosened them, and Tex, and expert knot-tier himself, undid the knot around his ankles. He was finally able to stand up, and the three looked at each other smiling. Sunita gave Jacob a quick kiss on the cheek, causing both he and Tex to blush in that room that no longer knew of any blushes, modesty or embarrassment. In a moment, they simultaneously realized their foolishness for waiting in the Hall for even a second longer than necessary. Jacob whispered, "Come on," and started to jog across the hall and down the passageway. Sunita and Tex followed immediately, both of them scared, relieved, and wondering how Phoebe had tied up Jacob and why she had left him there.

They didn't talk to each other until they were well outside the building, away from the danger of death, and the smells of orgiastic sex, away from the stifling odor of musty books and stale air-conditioned air. Sitting on the steps outside of the Library, Jacob sat down, and Sunita sat beside him, and Tex beside her.

"We'll be safe out here for a little while," Jacob said, already feeling a little relieved.

"Are you O.K.? Do you want to go to the hospital?"

"I'm O.K., Sunita, really. I don't need to go to any hospital. I've just got a few bruises, a little rope burn. Nothing a little bactin wouldn't help."

"Let's go to my place. I'll fix you up, and we can call the police from there...We have to go to the police!" Sunita

exclaimed. "We have to go!" Jacob and Tex nodded affirma-
tively. Tex was beginning to feel pangs of guilt for disliking
Jacob, and intended to make it up to him by helping Sunita
with the first-aid.

"Well, partner, looks like it was a close call," Tex said,
offering friendship. "What happened back there?"

"Let's just talk about it at Sunita's. I'm a little shaken up. I
don't know if Phoebe's mixed up in this or not."

"Jacob, what are you talking about!"

"It wasn't Phoebe who tied me up, it was that bouncer—"

"What bouncer?"

"The one from the bhangra. Phoebe wasn't around at all.
I don't know what happened to her—Maybe he's done something to her."

"Oh, Jacob. Don't you see—she set you up! Let's get out
of her, and call the cops."

After walking down the Library steps and down the street,
they passed a middle-aged man in a finely tailored Italian suit,
cut from emerald green cotton cloth, with a yellow silk scarf
wrapped around his neck, walking in the opposite direction.
His single eyebrow was raised in frustration. Speaking into his
cellular phone, he pleaded, "Dr. Patel, please, Dr. Patel. I
think I am coming very close to something. Please, Dr. Patel,
just wait....I know you are paying a lot of money.....I understand your position, sir....Yes...Yes...But Dr. Patel, please...."
And after Mr. Finch was several feet clear of the threesome, he
turned around and stood for a second, remembering her, and
taking mental note of Jacob.

For her part, when she went by Mr. Finch and heard his
heated discussion with this Dr. Patel, Sunita thought to
herself, "We are everywhere and nowhere." But she didn't
share this reflection with Jacob, who she believed wouldn't
understand. Nor did she tell Tex, for he would only make it a
point for argument, for discussion, and not allow her to
inhabit that moment of bittersweet aloneness.

11.

Dirk left Jacob to investigate the noises coming from one of the back passageways. Phoebe's instructions were clear. No one was to be in the Library when Jacob arrived. Govind, who rarely ventured outside of its confines, was told to leave until six o'clock that evening, when the next orgy was scheduled. Dirk was to take care of Jacob. Tie him up. Put him in a sack. Put the sack in a box. Put the box in a delivery truck and then dump box, sack, and Jacob into a lake an hour or so outside of the city limits. And then return the truck to the rental agency so they could still get the deposit back. But now, Govind seemed to be lurking around in the Library. Dirk would have to chase him off, without letting him see Jacob. There were some things it was better that he didn't know about.

"Govind, hey, Govind," Dirk whispered down one of the hallways. He heard more sounds from behind a closed door. Scratches, perhaps even a whimper. And then, of all things, bird sounds. What? The hooting of an owl? What was Govind doing now? Dirk opened the door, and walked into the darkness. He waited for his eyes to adjust, but they wouldn't. Too dark. He took a few more steps. "Govind, what the hell are you doing in here? Meditating?" Dirk heard the door close behind him. Two matches were lit simultaneously in front of him, revealing pitiless faces, menacing eyes. The matches were used to light two torches, creating a sinister, flickering light in the empty storeroom.

"Who is this Govind?" The voice came from behind him. Dirk turned around to face four others. "Hmm? Who is this Govind you are looking for?" asked a man, with a lean face and a hooked nose, and long, henna-dyed hair, streaked with grey. Dirk looked down to the man's hands, and his long bony fingers. He was holding a long yellow silk cloth.

Phoebe sat cross-legged on the floor-mat of her apartment. She burned some incense, hoping it would calm her nerves. Why she felt so edgy, she didn't know. Things never seemed to go her way anymore. What was Dirk doing anyway? He was supposed to have called already. Maybe things would be set right this time. Jacob had to be punished. He killed Aloysius, so he had to die. It was simple. Jacob was a traitor. A power-hungry traitor. He wanted to stop her, to destroy her. But he wouldn't succeed. Dirk would see to that. Ah, Dirk. He wasn't so bad. But she missed Aloysius. Death seemed so final. She believed in reincarnation, of course, but how would she know Aloysius when he came back? The ostensible goal of every yogi is to escape *samsara*, the endless cycle of births and deaths. Aloysius wasn't ready for that. There would be no liberation for him. She would miss him dearly when she attained nirvana. Perhaps in his next life he might attain salvation. It would take power, tremendous power—would he be able to achieve such strength again?

What a fool Jacob was! To have tried to stop her! She missed him too, in a strange way. He had gone bad, but he hadn't always been so. She had to punish him. There was no backing away from that, though she did feel sorry for him. He was so foolish. Why should he try to hurt her when she tried to teach him so much?

The telephone rang. "It must be Dirk," she thought and picked up. "Hello."

"It is done, Miss, just as you asked." It wasn't Dirk.

"Who is this? What are you talking about?"

"Miss Keli, you don't recognize me, your humble servant? I have always done everything you have asked, as well as I could. We have killed the large one. He was a strong man, but no match for the soldiers of Kali."

"You killed Dirk, you bastard?"

"Yes, Miss. We have sacrificed him to the Goddess. I do not see why you question the honor of my mother. We only followed your orders. We killed him, just as you asked. Just like you asked us to kill that angry one."

"What are you saying? I never asked you to do any such thing. I wanted Jacob dead. Only Jacob, not Dirk. And not Aloysius!"

"We will take care of him, too, Miss, as you wish, like the others. Your will shall prevail! We have disposed of the body properly, in the ancient fashion. We have cut him to pieces and buried him, breaking through the earth with the sacred pickaxe. We shall make no more mistakes as we do your bidding. It was quite difficult carving through—"

She hung up the phone.

This was not going to stop her. She had an orgy at six o'clock. She needed to get ready. It was an important one, the yogic forces were building within everyone, and she needed to tap into that collective flow to increase her own power, and bring her one step closer. Every day brought her closer to her goal. She would leave her mark upon her devotees. They would spread her teachings throughout the world, while she lived between earthly existence and the heavenly status of the fully liberated yogi. Her senses would encompass the world as she felt every leaf of every tree fall to the earth, the tears of anguish of every lonely child, and the pleasures of every man and woman who made love. Her words would be on the lips of thousands. Dirk's death would not stop her. Nor Aloysius's. Jacob would not interfere. She had an orgy to go to, and nothing would stop her.

Phoebe took a few minutes to do what any Tantric sex cult leader would do just before an orgy. She took a long hot bath, washed her hair, and lavished herself with high quality skin moisturizer. There would be time for stretching her muscles once she reached the Library. Properly stretched muscles were essential. An unwelcome muscle cramp could ruin hours of work. She began with a few forward bends, and touched her toes, and a couple other Western athlete's stretches. Then, she moved on to the appropriate preparatory yogic asanas, concentrating on the sacred breath all along. (Here, too, East met West). Now that she was sufficiently clean and the moisture sealed into her skin, she took a seat in her living room to rest and collect her thoughts.

Phoebe closed her eyes. She breathed in deeply and slowly, concentrating on that all-pervasive, ever-powerful syllable "OM." It had been a long time since she had meditated in what seemed now such a simple fashion. She too had been a student of the Librarian, and whatever her struggles and plans were now, the bond of guru and *chela* could not be fully broken. She would try to speak to him, to find some comfort.

She cleared her mind. She had to empty thoughts of Aloysius, easing herself of the tension that his memory caused. She wanted her thoughts of him to drift away with each exhalation of her breath, but his image reappeared: his body close to hers when they made love, his passion and his anger. She saw his flesh burning, the impossible, indescribable pain as he died in a street alleyway. But all was to be breathed away, to be freed from the body. Her breaths came further and further apart. Inhale. Exhale. Inhale. Exhale. The ancient, irrefutable rhythm of life. She felt herself soaring, weightless, borne aloft by her own breath. She saw Dirk, his tremendous body, flaccid, lifeless, and she almost plunged to earth. But she breathed deeply, regaining her strength, soaring ever higher. She saw Jacob, and she remembered him, their intimacy, and almost feeling regret, she began to descend. She would not allow it. Inhale. Exhale. Inhale. Exhale. She floated up and up, and into darkness, starless darkness.

She concentrated upon her teacher. Thinking of his benevolent smile, his intelligent, piercing eyes. She focused all her mental energies, desperately trying to come close to him, wishing to hear his voice, to speak with him. Would he provide wisdom and guidance in this moment of need? Would he speak to her? Would he answer her call? He did not.

"What had happened to Phoebe, with all her promise, her passion, and all her power?" Sunita would ask, seated at the Cafe Feu d'Amour along with Jacob and Tex, two months after the dissolution of the Order and the arrest of all alleged murderers. "Things seemed to have moved far beyond her control. Events were directed by a malevolent intelligence. Someone or something outside of herself. The ancient Indians, or really, it was the Brahmin orthodoxy, who didn't much care for the Tantrikas, whatever it was they were doing, believed that the practice of the yogic arts by a woman was tantamount to witchcraft. The release of the feminine force, so they said, required a male force in order to properly harness it. Without the male principle, the female shakti would spin wildly out of control. Witchcraft. Was this what happened to Phoebe? Had she dared to enter the world of yoga as a mere woman? Was she nothing more than a witch?" Tex knew better than to answer the question, and Jacob was quite enjoying Sunita's excursus. "What a bunch of patriarchal nonsense! The practices of yoga were kept away from women to enhance and maintain a patriarchal social structure. Having said that, what happened to Phoebe?" Sunita inadvertently gestured to push up reading glasses, which she happened not to be wearing, up to the bridge of her nose. (She had lost them at least a year ago). "Clearly something besides witchery. Something within her short-circuited, rendering her incapable of trust, and scared of anyone who might threaten her tentative hold upon herself. But what was it? And did it matter whatever 'it' was...."

After rescuing Jacob and returning to her apartment, Sunita called the police to report an assault and battery, kidnapping, conspiracy and downright dishonesty and meanness all connected to the murders of Ephraim Stockwell and Aloysius Caine. She was put on hold. When she finally reached the detective supposedly handling the case, she told her story, or really, Jacob's story. She tried to share her conspiracy theory, but was interrupted at least six times with "Ma'am, please." After she had finished, the detective asked

her where exactly Jacob was at this moment, since Sunita had
not at any point relinquished the phone to him. Told to stay
where they were, and not to return to Jacob's apartment under
any circumstances, the three Defenders of Justice waited for
someone to come to take Jacob's statement. "Apparently,"
Sunita told Tex and Jacob after getting off the phone, "the
cops are on to the cult, and they've been keeping Phoebe
under surveillance. They even knew that Dirk was mixed up
in all of this somehow. They're going to make arrests soon,
and they want our help to confirm the identity of the suspects—and Jacob, they want you to testify for the prosecution
when this thing goes to trial."

About an hour and half after Sunita's phone call to the
police, someone knocked on the front door. Tex and Jacob
froze. Sunita leaped up and ran to the door. Closing one eye,
she squinted through the other so she could look through the
peephole. She was a little surprised to see a face that she
recognized. She actually recognized not an entire face, but an
eyebrow—the singular, furry eyebrow of Private Detective
Mortimer Aspen Finch. Was he another member of the cult?
Had Phoebe sent him? Sunita called out, "Who is it?" A
badge was held in front of the peephole. "Police, ma'am."
When she finally managed to unlock the two dead bolts and
unfasten the chain, Sunita saw that the hand that held out the
badge belonged to an arm covered in grey, while the eyebrow
she recognized was part of a face that was attached to a body
covered in an emerald green suit. There were two men. One
a police detective, and the other, a private one. A well-con-
nected, friends-in-the-force-private detective who received a
phone call relaying Sunita's conversation as soon as she hung
up the phone. Introductions were made, and Jacob and
Sunita sat on the chairs she dragged in from the kitchen, while
Tex, Finch and the other detective sat on the couch.

Why had a phone call to the city's finest led to the appearance of a private detective hired to investigate the bhangra
murder? The police had more or less left the case to
Mortimer, and were now only following his lead. No questions of jurisdiction were raised, no egos battled for power: it

was his intuition, his clues, his case. He was the one who was monitoring Phoebe, he was the one who was on to the cult, he was the one who put some credence in the fantastic theories of a lonely scholar deprived the company of his best pupil. And Mortimer was the one who knew about the brawny bouncer, though he didn't know he was a bouncer. The police possessed only the sketchiest of details, though Mortimer told his contact to send officers to the Library that evening at six o'clock to make arrests. What? The police taking orders from a private citizen? To avoid complications from that issue—complications always arose when the media was involved, and they were invited to witness the spectacle—Finch was accompanied to Sunita's by the grey-suited detective. He knew very little about the case, though he did know quite a bit about the high esteem in which Finch was held by the old guard in the department. He said nothing during the interview. Everyone who needed to knew that this case was "Finch's baby." That acknowledged ownership was quite important to Mortimer. He would solve another case, earn another solid gold reference, and further his legendary status among the detectives of both the private and police variety. No junior detective would dare to interfere in that. Sit silently and learn was all that was to be expected.

Tex insisted, however, that the silent cop repeatedly looked him over with great suspicion and unmistakable dislike, to which Sunita replied, "It's because you were spitting into that cup, Tex! What a vile and disgusting habit!" But Tex's excessive expectoration was not simply a matter of Lubbockian manners, or a lack thereof. He was nervous. Having faced the dangers of a murderous sex cult, albeit from a twice removed position (Jacob was obviously first in line to be offed, and Sunita had to be somewhere after him), Tex now sat in a room with the gun-toting representatives of secular authority. And he hadn't a clue how much Jacob would reveal. A magical book? Ancient Hindu spells cast by a grandfatherly guru? All three of them would be locked away...

Jacob left out only a few details when he told his story to Finch. No mention was made of the Book and its extraordinary abilities, much to both Sunita and Tex's relief. How would they look if they had followed around a slightly deluded former cult member? He was a "former cult member" wasn't he? Jacob, of course, was anxious too. He knew the stakes—he knew what could and couldn't be said. He certainly didn't feel it necessary to reveal everything about his final rendezvous with the Librarian. It would only detour the investigation. Besides, no one else really knew what happened between Jacob and his guru that night, except Phoebe and Aloysius, who really only made educated guesses. And neither one, for very different reasons, would do any talking. Jacob told Finch that the old man had passed away, but that he didn't know if the appropriate agencies had been notified. He assumed that Phoebe and Aloysius must have in some way disposed of the body. It shocked Jacob himself that he had so easily forgotten about the old man, but well, "You see, the Librarian's spirit still lived on with me. It was hard to think of him as dead," he explained, and so, it was quite easy to overlook such details. Mind over body and all that. The police officer scrawled a note. Finch would discover a few hours later that the old man had been cremated, Phoebe having instructed Govind to handle the arrangements. Certified cause of death: cardiac arrest. What kind of foul play was to be suspected when a library janitor reported the death of a lonely, old librarian, who had passed away with a smile on his face?

Sunita made some coffee, and Jacob rolled a cigarette. At the bhangra, Jacob continued, he had begun to feel quite strangely, and speculated that his meditation session with the Librarian, not to mention the arrival of Aloysius at Phoebe's apartment, must have drained him of his energy much more than he thought. Or, he had to admit, he might have been drugged. Sunita nodded her head. At this point, Tex chimed in to explain the finer points of South Asian diaspora subcultures, producing a cassette tape of the newest bhangra mix as Exhibit A, and still found time to let on that he had quite a reputation on the bhangra bull-riding circuit. No official note was made of Tex's accomplishment. Sunita was certain that Phoebe had given Jacob some kind of sense-dulling chemical.

"What else could explain that kind of behavior? I mean, he wasn't drunk, I've seen plenty of drunk people, and Jacob was not drunk. Clearly a conspiracy between Dirk and Phoebe to get rid of Jacob." Finch was impressed by the beautiful, young amateur detective, and said so. One might say that he gushed praise, which Tex would in fact remark later. But Mortimer was curious as to why Phoebe had any motivation to kill Jacob in the first place. (He was probing for any indication of less-than-innocent involvement on Jacob's part. His assertion that, "Yes, I was in the Order, but not really in it. I mostly just went there for what was really a kind of private tutoring on Eastern philosophy and yoga," seemed quite possible, though also had the tone of a constructed alibi to Finch's ears). Before Jacob could offer his hypothesis, Sunita exclaimed, "Power! She's after Power, and Jacob was a threat! He was the favorite of the old leader, and though he didn't know it, he was resented by the others." Finch was impressed. Sunita was pleased with herself. Tex was getting bored and hungry. And the police detective, for the most part apparently disinterested, stared at Sunita's chest, which heaved dramatically when she shouted "Power!" Did Finch ever suspect Jacob of any role in the murders? Was he certain that the bookish young man was telling the entire story? Finch's preternatural senses were not aroused. Perhaps Jacob was protected by Sunita's aura, which, given Finch's immediate predilection for her, prevented any super-sensory verification of Jacob's statement.

Much more had to be explained. Finch found all the details quite interesting, though already all signs pointed to Phoebe's guilt, which was effectively the truth. Jacob told how he met Sunita and Tex, and how they extended their friend-ship at a time of need. It all sounded rather pathetic to Finch, though Sunita was touched, and Tex was too, but he didn't want to show it. (It wasn't that he didn't know how to show it, it was more that he knew that it was better to look like he didn't know how. Especially in front of the authorities). And just how did Jacob get mixed up in this again? He received a phone call from Phoebe, who insisted that they meet. When he returned to the Library, he was accosted by Dirk, but was luckily saved from bodily injury, or even death, by Tex and Sunita in a daring rescue. Finch looked to Sunita. She beamed.

"And then we decided it was time to call the police."

"Tell me something, Jacob. If you even had a hunch that Phoebe Keli was out to get you—why did you endanger yourself a second time?" asked Finch.

"I was never certain, and I'm not one hundred per cent certain now, though Sunita keeps telling me that I'm letting myself be deceived. I still believe in her. It's something, I guess, about the nature of love," Jacob answered. There was not much more to be said after that. Though an eyebrow was raised, as if saying, "Love? If that's what you want to call it...."

As he and his police sidekick were preparing to leave, Finch reminded the threesome of the six o'clock arrest, and again extended an invitation. He paused, thoughtfully, looked around the room and lifted his eyebrow for the third time during the session. Jacob, Sunita and Tex simultaneously felt a twinge of a fear. Did Finch know that Jacob had withheld a few pieces of information here and there in the telling of the tale? "I can't say that I've never come across the combination of sex and murder in my line of work. But this...ah, it really is no different from the rest....Thanks very much for your cooperation." He smiled at Sunita, "And thank you, Ms. Chid-um-, Chid-um, um... Thanks for being such a wonderful hostess during this indubitably stressful time."

With the door shut, and Finch and police officer away and down the hall, or in the elevator, or in the very least, Somewhere Else, the three would-be crimefighters slouched down in the couch. They said nothing to one another, each feeling strangely conspiratorial. Jacob had to leave out certain details to make himself sound credible, Tex and Sunita assured themselves. And though not entirely certain how much he kept hidden, they both knew that he must have kept even more secrets, and knew that they had helped him keep them from the Law.

"Well, y'all," Tex said, breaking the silence, "we'd better giddy up if we're goin' to make this thing by six."

12.

$\mathcal{T}$ime: 5:55 pm. Location: Phoebe's Library office, located in one of the passageways leading away from the Hall of Cubicles. Not very far, in fact, from the site of Dirk's demise. Phoebe was burdened with an unwelcome guest. Hooked Nose Ameer. She glanced at the clock as he spoke. The orgy was scheduled to begin at six, and it would be quite bad for morale were she late. But Ameer would have none of it. He had come to speak to Phoebe, and he was determine that he be heard. He served her well up until now, did her bidding, and indeed, fulfilled her wishes without her even asking him.

Six o'clock. Phoebe and Ameer could hear the beginnings of the orgy. Oohs and Aahs and whimpers of pleasure. Only newer members made such noises. Those further along in their training maintained much greater control.

"With all due respect, Miss, things seemed to have changed quite a bit here."

"Changed? What do you mean?"

"All this hanky-panky."

"We are only following the path set by our departed master."

"It is a little unclean, Miss, a little unclean."

"Are you suggesting that I—that I am ritually impure?"

"Oh, no, not at all, Miss. I would never even dream such a thing. You are so powerful. So knowing. It is for you to say what is pure and impure. As it is for you to say who shall live and who shall die."

"What do you mean by that?"

"I see, you are testing me. Testing my devotion. What do I mean? I mean that we have killed the two that you have commanded me to kill."

"I never asked you to kill Aloysius. Or Dirk. Only Jacob, which you managed not to do. Now, get out of here, I have to go out there..." Ameer moved in front of the door to block Phoebe's exit.

"I think you should wait here for a minute. Wait and speak to me." She looked into his hateful eyes. The eyes of a killer. "I am your servant, Miss. As your loyal servant, I have some requests to make of you." Eyes of hate became eyes of lust. "I have always obeyed. You wished for these others to be destroyed as a sacrifice to the Mother. And I obeyed your word. You wished it, and I heard your wish. The wind whispered your deepest desires to me, and I heard them. I have killed for you."

"It's not true! I never wanted to hurt them...What have you done?"

"Come to me, Miss. These hands have killed for you. They are yours. Kiss them."

Phoebe looked down to his bony fingers, his aged hands, and staring at them, she saw the silk scarf, as Dirk had seen it, as Aloysius had seen it. "Come, Ms. Keli, come to me..."

It was with his final "come" that screams and shouts could be heard from the great hall. Ameer became distracted, the spell was broken. Phoebe shouted, "Something's gone wrong out there!" and rushed for the door.

Jacob, Sunita and Tex stood outside of the Library, per Mortimer Finch's instructions. Just before six o'clock, but no sooner, and certainly not any later. Finch loved an audience. Besides Sunita, he had also tipped off his favorite television reporter. A television news van was parked in the street, and reporter Jack Flanagan along with his cameraman stood waiting for the action to begin. The police had to be there before they could start the camera rolling. At three minutes to six, Finch arrived, donned in his preferred outfit for meeting new clients and major busts: horse-riding gear, with crop tucked under his arm. At two minutes to six, three unmarked police cars, each filled with four plain clothes detectives arrived. And at one minute to six, three squad cars arrived with uniformed officers.

Jack Flanagan turned on his smile and began to speak into his microphone, "We are here awaiting the arrest of members of a murderous cult that practices bizarre sexual rituals. They are led by one Phoebe Keli, who we understand is to be charged with ordering the murders of Ephraim Stockwell and Aloysius Caine...."

At thirty seconds to six o'clock, three brown Mercedes-Benzes pulled up, each carrying members of the elite squadron of Aunties assigned to the case since the murder at the bhangra. In addition to their bright pink salwar-kameezes, they each wore American police-issue riot headgear, purchased from a local Army-Navy surplus store. Each Auntie also carried Indian police-issue lathi sticks, to be used on the heads of the decadent culties. Long on Phoebe's trail, they had pursued the case with great tenacity and secrecy. Neither the police nor Private Detective Finch knew of their covert operations. It would soon take eight police officers and the threat of arrest to restrain the militants, who wished nothing other than to rush the Library and bash some heads in the name of Modesty and Decency.

One of the Aunties caught sight of Sunita and called out, "Sooo-nita! Sooo-nita Sunita Chidhambaram! Is that you? What are you doing here, dear?"

Sunita refused to turn around. She recognized the voice. And she knew the consequences of her act of defiance: First would come the harrying phone calls of her mother. Then, when she visited home, whispers and false smiles at all of the functions and social occasions. Little protection would her armor of salwar kamiz or sari offer against suburban Indian-American gossip were she to be placed on the Aunties' list. "Soo-nita! Soo-nita!" she cried, but Sunita held firm, refusing to yield, breaking thousands upon thousands of years of tradition, shaking a fist at the edifice of Asian discipline and family values. She would not surrender. No, she would not.

She was in control of her life, her destiny, her sexuality, her career.

"Oh, hi, Nachu Auntie. How are you?" Sunita said meekly and watched as her name was recorded into the Aunties' book of miscreants. Tex smiling wickedly, taking pleasure in Sunita's plight, arrogantly turned to face the gang of Aunties. He did not fear them. This particular group was headquartered far from the Houston-Dallas axis that patrolled his fellow Indo-Lubbockians.

"Anil Chadha! *Aray bachha*! *Thu itha kee kheer ay a*!" How did they know? The Aunties had finally overcome their regional differences. Midwest reached out to the West Coast, East Coast to the Southwest. They functioned now as a single unit, and Tex's mug shot and rap sheet had indeed been reviewed in the local chapter. Tex waved, vainly hoping that his gender might provide some immunity from retribution. At least some time would be bought before his parents were informed, since they were now touring the New Mexico desert in their motorhome, which Sunil had recently purchased for them.

Phoebe ran down the passageway into the Great Hall. Ameer followed her, shouting "Miss, Miss! Wait! Come back!" He stopped suddenly and his face turned dark red. Phoebe had run into the arms of Mortimer Finch, who quickly pulled out a set of handcuffs and informed her of her arrest for the murder of Ephraim Stockwell and Aloysius Caine. Ameer felt a strong arm upon his shoulder, and turned to see the unsympathetic face of a plain-clothes police officer.

A distraught Phoebe pointed to an even more disturbed Ameer, whose face, at the moment when Mortimer's gaze fell upon him, exchanged the deep red hue of embarrassment for the deathly pale of guilt and fear. "He's the one!" she screamed. "He's the one who killed Aloysius and Dirk!"

Rubber-gloved police officers untangled the bodies of the cult members, still locked together in intricate sexual positions, and all in a heightened state of sensitivity. They responded to each push and pull of the stiff hand of Authority with a groan of pleasure. The feel of latex gloves against their skin sent them only into further and further rapture. It was only when cult members were pulled away from the pile of bodies and felt the cold steel of handcuffs upon their wrists that their orgiastic trances were broken. Charged en masse with public acts of lewdness, the cult members hooted and hollered in protest, and several required a swift strike with a baton just in case they felt sufficiently aggrieved to riot.

Phoebe and Ameer were kept aside as the rank and file were led out one by one into the waiting police vans. Unlucky Govind, too, was kept aside. He had not taken part in the orgy, and a crime for which he could be charged was quickly being decided upon. Govind had been set out to stand watch by Phoebe, and indeed, he saw the police on their way to bust the cult. But Govind had let himself go of late, especially since being banned from the orgies by Phoebe, and he found the dash to the secret hiding place nearly impossible to complete at a pace rapid enough to outrun Finch and his colleagues. He had more or less led them straight to the hideout, as they followed the sounds of his wheezing and panting, and occasionally caught a glimpse of his nearly naked body waddling down the sparsely lit passageways.

Govind had managed to earn Finch's pity, and Ameer's disdain. Phoebe reserved her hatred for Ameer, and as soon as the noise had subsided in the hall—first came the moans of pleasure, then the shouts of protest, followed by cries of pain—Phoebe willingly confessed to Mortimer, hoping to implicate Ameer as quickly and efficiently as possible. She didn't care what happened to her, she told Finch. But she wanted this bastard Ameer to hang. He was a killer, a fiend, a devil. He and his entire cult.

Finch suspended judgment on the distribution of guilt between Phoebe and Ameer. It wasn't unknown for one partner in crime to turn upon the other in the moment of defeat at the hands of Justice. Besides, details like this were for the district attorney's office to sort out. Finch, though, had indeed developed something of a prurient interest in Phoebe, and certainly wished that a greater share of the blame was

Ameer's. What piqued Finch's interest even more than Phoebe's body robed in a loose silk was her mention of another cult. A through and through secularist –he would never openly admit agnosticism or atheism– Finch had enjoyed his part in smashing the religious extremism of Phoebe's "OM"-chanting killer sex-a-holics, and the prospect of exposing another bunch of fanatics was very appealing. And they really could be the true murderers of Caine and Stockwell, and Dirk. Dirk, too?

"Did you say that they killed Dirk, that man who has frequently accompanied you to the Cafe Feu d'Amour?"

"Dirk was my bodyguard....and my lover. And they killed him," Phoebe responded.

"So, this Ameer was in the business of killing your lovers....interesting."

"We have just seen the removal of the cult members from their secret hideaway, which we understand we will have access to once the area is secured. What a procession of smut-minded perverts we have here....They look like they could be your next-door neighbor, your doctor, your teacher, a local musician, and yet they've sought their God through the most inhumane of means..."

"Will y'all look at that!" drawled Tex.

"There's so many of them. I never realized. I mean, I saw them all, but never like this."

Sunita remained silent, as she watched the cult members being brought out and taken into the police vans. After the final few were packed away to be taken to the station house, and all of the police vans had driven away, it was time for Phoebe and Harry to be brought out.

"We understand that there were two leaders to the cult, a husband and wife team, it may very well be..." The voice of the television reporter drifted to Sunita's ears—"husband and wife team" lodging themselves in her earwax. "What bullshit!" she said aloud.

Ameer came first, his hands cuffed behind him, his head bowed to hide his face from the crowd of newspaper, television

and radio reporters who had arrived on the scene once Jack
Flanagan had gone on the air. And then came Phoebe, beautiful, sad Phoebe, handcuffed, head held high. Piercing black
eyes surveyed the scene, the reporters, the onlookers. Jacob.
Sunita. Phoebe looked away, and spoke the sacred mantra to
herself, and waited to be borne away from this place, from
these cuffs, from police and reporters, and lovers and murderers. She was led to an unmarked police car, and was driven
away.

Sunita had watched her leave the Library, and walk down
the stairs to the sidewalk, and she met Phoebe's eyes. Sunita
watched her get into the car, and she watched her be taken
away. She walked toward the space where the car had been,
leaving Jacob and Tex behind. She stood and watched as the
sedan turned the corner. She felt sad for Phoebe. Sad, but she
had been right. Phoebe had to be stopped. She had become
something other than who she was.

Jacob too had followed Phoebe with his eyes. And the
gaze of her penetrating, yet he thought, hollow eyes. But as he
turned to watch her enter the police car, Sunita blocked his
view. And it made him smile to see Sunita, to see her there
because now she was a part of his life. She was beautiful,
strong, intelligent, so much what he had dreamed of and
longed for. They would settle things, find a way to make it all
work.

As Sunita stood watching the sedan drive away, the open
shirt she was wearing over her tank top was caught in the
wind, and dropped down revealing her bare shoulder. Jacob
squinted, thinking he saw something on her back. A mark of
some kind...He strained his eyes, trying to see the shape...A
tattoo...maybe...was there really something there?...two almond shaped eyes, with two wavy lines above them –could he
be imagining this?– they must have been eyebrows...and a
nose, yes, a nose like a question mark. And in the center of
what would be the forehead of the face, there was a small,
shaded mark....She felt prying, almost unfriendly eyes on her
back, and so lifted her shirt back over her shoulder. She
turned around to see whose forceful gaze had been upon her.